Love Maxed Out

Joseph Harris

Copyright © 2018 Joseph Harris

Editing & Cover Design by

Destiny House Publishing, LLC

P.O. Box 19774

Detroit, MI 48219

www.destinyhousepublishing.com

email: inquiry@destinyhousepublishing

All rights reserved.

ISBN-13: 978-1936867332

ISBN-10:1936867338

DEDICATION & INSPIRATION:

I thank God for my parents who introduced me to Jesus and my baptism as a child. My father, Joe Arthur Doyle and my mother, Gussie Doyle were responsible for my life. I thank God for having parents that loved me and always demonstrated it to me. I am inspired to write this book because of the love of Jesus Christ, the love of my parents and my wife. My parents are now in the presence of the Lord in Heaven. Thank you, Jesus, my Lord, Savior and Redeemer.

CONTENTS

Page

	Acknowledgments	i
	Introduction	1
1	Love Maxed Out	3
2	Created to Love	10
3	The Love Compass	19
4	The Anointed One	25
5	Perfect Love	28
6	Positioned to Love	31
7	The Miracle Maker	40
8	Champion of Love	50
9	Your Body A Temple	58
10	A True Christian Soldier	69

11	Devotion and Honor	77
12	Love is patient, Love is Kind	87
13	The Love GPS (Global Positioning System)	92
14	Church is The Treatment Center	99
15	Take Your Life Back	114
16	Moses, The Man of God	120
17	Nothing Separates You from the Love of God	130
18	Love in Every Heartbeat	135
19	God Is Love	146

ACKNOWLEDGMENTS

Thanks to my heavenly Father, Jesus Christ and the Holy Ghost for blessing me and keeping me. Thanks to my parents, Joe Arthur Doyle and Gussie Doyle for their consistent and dedicated love. I thank my parents for introducing me to the Lord, Jesus Christ. Thanks to my wife for constant love and support. Thanks to all my siblings, friends and the church. Thanks to the Destiny House Publishing team.

INTRODUCTION

This book is designed to help people accept Jesus Christ as Lord and Savior as they experience His love. Please note that the Bible is the word of God containing the unlimited love of God. There is no substitution, nor anything in all of creation that can compare. In His Love, the power of grace, mercy and forgiveness exist. Jesus is the only one that gives compassion, healing, and comfort to restore and make whole again.

Love is the focus throughout this book inspired by God's word and His revelation knowledge. This book touches on several areas of love that people deal with daily. It also opens a multitude of helpful pointers and makes every believer and non-believer aware of God's power. Being an agent and ambassador of Jesus warrants all of us saints to follow His command to love (Matthew 22:36-37). Therefore, we should make every effort to spread God's love and the Good News (Gospel) throughout the world in the best way possible to all people. By spreading the Word of God, we demonstrate a major action in maxing out God's love. It is because we are Kingdom people. We do understand that maxing out God's love really means to use all the love that God gives you toward others to win them to Christ. This will impact their lives, by pushing them towards transformation and bring them into the blessed life. It is already understood and clear that God's love is unlimited. The notion and effort to max out implies that we should use what God gives in every situation and circumstance to reveal that its God's love manifested through you by Him. This does not mean that His love runs out because it is impossible for God to exhaust His love. He never has to resupply! He is the supplier of love! God is love and He is the God who first loved us (1 John 4:8, 16, 19).

Accepting Jesus as Lord and Savior is a vital step in receiving God's love. Love maxed out does not suggest that your love is exhausted. Love maxed out means that you are putting forth the maximum effort in loving everyone. Every time He blesses someone with salvation, deliverance, or healing, he is revealing and demonstrating the power of love! You must become a child of God. It is really a life and death choice. The power of love can save a person's life. If you do not know Jesus, start by asking Him to come into your heart right now, repent of your sin and believe His words in Romans 10:9-10 then you are born again. This one decision and step in your life can alter the course of your life and thousands of others.

This book is written to point each person to the power of true love, which is God. It is to reveal the absolute incredible and unfailing love of God daily in all circumstances. It's about you intentionally receiving and giving your best love to Jesus Christ from the heart and to the people you meet. Love is power, and people need love to live with one another on this planet. Show the best love inside your heart to others. It might be difficult at times, but you can do it in Jesus name. The best love you have is from Jesus Christ! Pray right now and show fifty people either each week, month or at least within 6 months or a year the love of Jesus Christ (John 3:16). The scripture encourages us to "Be a doer of the word (James 1:22)" Let someone know who Jesus is and what He has done in your life. Ask God to make you a fisher of men (Mark 4). Become a permanent witness and do it face to face, if you can. If you are unable to do it face to face, use social media (such as Facebook, Twitter, cell phone, email or by any other means. Husbands, wives and mothers, this book is a must read regarding your marriage, sons, and daughters and the blessing of the Lord on your life.

CHAPTER 1

LOVE MAXED OUT

John 3:16 For God so loved the world, that he gave his only begotten Son, that whosoever believeth in him should not perish, but have everlasting life.

A 14 years old boy went in for surgery after discovering a huge lump on his body, along with Hypothyroidism causing the body to dysfunction. The lump was caused by extreme straining of muscle tissue. Prior to the surgery, the surgeon had realized that the hospital did not have the blood on hand for this young boy. The doctors explained to his mother that they did not have a blood match available and this surgery was needed now or else this child would suffer longer and could have further complications or even result in death. Not realizing that she already had what her son needed, she was advised to tell her husband to come to hospital at a critical stage while on the sick bed. As soon as the father finished working, he headed for the hospital. This hard laboring construction worker was responsible and accountable to ensure foundations and footings along with the necessary reinforcement bars were in place at one site. He also had to ensure that the bricks were installed properly at another site. On top of that, he was responsible for ensuring key interior and exterior jobs were on track for three separate million-dollar projects at three additional locations.

Nevertheless, he rushed to his wife and son at the hospital. The doctors told her repeatedly they could not locate any blood with his type. When the father understood what his son needed, he asked the doctor, "Can my son use my blood?! The doctor ran tests and the answer was "Yes it's a match!" The expression of joy on the mother's face was more than any amount of money could buy. They started the procedure of the blood transfusion. Immediately, the son came back to life. He had been in a coma and declared brain dead. For several weeks. He needed his father's blood to survive. It was the right blood type. His blood system was so close to what His Father had that it amazed the doctors. One doctor thought it to be rare. All the doctors, surgeon team, and family members all applauded and praised God when they heard the news that it was a success!

It is powerful to have a father who can show up and give love to his son by means of blood. This is what God did when He gave His Son, Jesus to save the world. Jesus' blood is much more than a match! His blood has all power inside of it! His blood washed us whiter than snow! Jesus was given to all of mankind as the perfect sacrifice. Jesus was called the Lamb of God that God used to take away the sin of the world. When we think of Jesus, we should automatically think on Him giving us new life by the power of His blood infusion.

Listen, the 12-year-old son is now well passed his 50 years of age and married with children, planted a church and preaching the gospel of Jesus Christ. He believed in his father and now he believes in Jesus Christ enough to serve Him whole heartedly! I am so thankful for my father's blood and how God used him to change my life when I was on the sick bed, half dead. My father's blood was used for my blood transfusion.

I live today because my father showed the power of love by making himself a sacrifice by giving up his blood when I was hospitalized and needed several pints of blood. My father made it on time. God sent Jesus to be the sacrifice and the source of life for all people in the world. God gave His best! Jesus is the best and the only way to max out every good thing! Jesus is God's only begotten Son! His blood covers all sin for those who believe on Him. His blood has power to restore life. His blood demonstrated the power of love. Within His blood is the power to heal anything in the name of Jesus. Love maxed out is not the end of His love and power. Love maxed out is written to prove that Jesus' love never ends and is unlimited in power and He is love! Love maxed is not to be interpreted as though all of God's love is used up. His love is never used up. His love has more power than anything. His love is the reason that the universe exists. His love created it!

Nothing is impossible for Him! Jesus is available right now for you! Ask Jesus to come into your heart right now! Nothing is stopping you! Ask Jesus to remove any barriers! He has the power to move Satan and demons out of your life. He has the power to restore your life and put you back on the right path of life! Let Jesus inside of your heart right now! Believe in Him! You will never regret it! Listen believe in Jesus so you will have eternal life. Believe in Jesus so you will help save another soul.

GOD GAVE HIS BEST!

Luke 23:32-33 And there were also two other, malefactors, led with him to be put to death. And when they were come to the place, which is called Calvary, there they crucified him, and the malefactors, one on the right hand, and the other on the left.

Love is the most important thing given and received! God gave His very best love to the entire world in order than they will receive eternal life. God's best Love is Jesus, the sacrifice for all people for the purpose and hope of love. Have you ever made sacrifices for your love? Yes! God's love is so powerful that it goes throughout the entire world touching lives daily. God's love matters the most because it affects every person, every living thing in all creation. His love covers all. God's love is maxed out in all His creation. There are no places in the world and universe that anyone can hide from the love of God. You are being loved even in difficult times in your life. God is still with you to see you through.

Everything you go through is not easily explained or it may not be explained at all, because of His mysterious ways. There are no hiding or secret places from His love. His love reaches the depths of all creation. His love is continuously active and is never shut off! You can turn a water faucet on and off. However, you can't turn Jesus' love off! Imagine His love being like a water hydrant constantly pouring out on your life daily. His love is in the atmosphere and every family and individual's life. If you want to know what love is, God is love.

The best love from God ever was and is His Son Jesus Christ who sits at the right hand of the Father in heaven. When the Father gave Jesus, He showed us what love maxed out looks like. God gave His son Jesus in the form of a sacrifice. He was placed on a cross and died for you and me (John 19). Jesus made a statement on the cross that no man can ever forget: Luke 23:34 records "Then said Jesus, Father, forgive them; for they know not what they do. And they parted his raiment, and cast lots. His forgiveness is the ultimate act of love and freedom. Never again should you walk in guilt and condemnation. Jesus broke that spell and power from your life! No one can match God's power of love and forgiveness. However, we are made to walk in it. Every time I find myself in a situation that stirs up something negative and ungodly, it is the Holy Spirit who pulls me back in to remember the power of love and forgiveness. Believe in Him today so you will not perish, instead have everlasting life. You will live with Jesus forever! Please receive this gift of love from God. It does not cost you anything. His love has the power to build and sustain our lives. The Holy Spirit is constantly showing us the love of God in this life. There is no escaping the love of God. No one should want less than God's love. 1 John 4:8 tells us that "God is love." All manner of love comes from Almighty God. If you are married, the love you have for your wife comes from God. The same applies to the husband from the wife. God ordained marriages to operate by love. Love is also mostly expressed in emotions between two people which deal with close relationships; such as in the marriage relationship. Love is so powerful God sent His Only Son to express love and used it to save a sinful and dying world that deserved God's wrath.

God unleashed His love when He sent Jesus to earth in the form of a human. He was sentenced to death by sinners namely Pontius Pilate, the Pharisees, and His own people. Jesus was sent to be a sacrifice to save all people from the wrath of God. The worst part, as explained to us in John 1:1-12, is that Jesus came to His own and they knew Him not. In others words, they turned their back on Jesus so that He could be crucified, even though He was innocent. Can you imagine the power behind rejection? Can you imagine the power behind turning your back on someone? When this happens in your life, ask the Lord to help you correct the situation, immediately. God's people rejected Jesus. But Jesus never rejected us nor turned His back on us. God had the perfect opportunity in the Garden of Eden because of our rebellious and disobedient nature. Jesus could have called down thousands of angels at one single thought to take out every person on this planet. His love for people stopped him. Love stopped that thought and love kept Jesus on the path of redeeming lost souls. God gave his only Son for me and you. What do we have to give God?

We should give of ourselves completely in service to God and whatever He asks. Because God's essence is love, He gave every human being the power of love inside the heart. No one else has the power to supply love and eternal life. This is love maxed out! In other words, it extends beyond our comprehension and ability.

In marriage, you can only love so much, there are human limitations. Nevertheless, there is an abundance of blessings in marriage, if you walk in obedience and true love. Make no mistake that marriage is a blessing because God created it.

There are several types of love: agape, phileo, and eros. The most powerful is agape love because nothing is required for it. You don't pay for it. It's not manipulated. There is no ring involved, no money, absolutely nothing. Agape love comes from God. You can never earn agape love. It is God's unconditional love. Agape love is total and complete love from God. Of course, all love comes from God. All categories of true love come from the creator of the universe. Erose means desiring and longing. This applies to sexual love. It is a selfish kind of love. This love is based on physical attraction. This love involves control as well. This type of love is found in couples and marriages. Sexual relations have a lot to do with driving the relationship. Agape love represents the kind of the love from Jesus. This is the best of love. Agape love is a love commanded by God. This kind of love does not deal with our feelings. This is the kind of love that believers experience from God. Conditional love is manipulation. Conditional love must be shut down by couples immediately when you notice it. An example of conditional love is when a person wants something in exchange for something they have or can give you. It can be as simple as sex for doing something around the house or she or he wants. A child can also engage in manipulation and play on your love. For example they may say, "Because I am your daughter purchase this $500.00 dress for me". Another example, "Because I am your only son purchase this new vehicle for me".

Phileo love refers to love toward a friend or person close and dear to you. Phileo love is a brotherly love. This is a love that believers also practice. The problem is that it is not reliable kind of love, instead it easily becomes difficult. Therefore, Agape love is the most powerful. You do not work for Agape love. The "Passion of the Christ" movie gives us such a powerful picture of love in action and pouring out by Jesus dying on the cross. The idea is to paint the picture of Jesus maxed out love to save us by giving His life on the cross. It helps to reveal the ultimate meaning of love. When it comes to the cross and the resurrection, it's because of love. I must admit with a heart of Jesus Christ that the demonstration of love maxed out was revealed at that very moment and again when Jesus rose from the grave (resurrection). In fact, there is no greater love than this, Jesus laid down His life for me, you, and every person in the world.

Questions and discussion:

1. Why is John 3:16 so important to you?

_____

2. List and explain each type of love.

_____
_____
_____

3. What do these three types of love describe?

_____
_____
_____

4. What kind of love is the most important that comes from God?

_____

5. Is conditional love earned? Why/Why not?

_____

6. What does His love mean to you? Why?

_____
_____

CHAPTER 2

CREATED TO LOVE

GENESIS 2:7 And the Lord God formed man of the dust of the ground, and breathed into his nostrils the breath of life; and man became a living soul. GENESIS 2:18 And the Lord God said, It is not good that the man should be alone; I will make him an help meet for him.

It is important to not entertain these movies that I am about to mention to you because our adversary wants these evil movies etched into your spirit man to destroy you! A movie of the century that many people watched is called "Frankenstein." As a young boy, I watched this movie along with my siblings out of interest and entertainment because it was a crazy monster picture and we wanted to see it. It's crazy how human beings really desire to see horror movies. The problem was our curiosity overwhelmed us so much that the enemy deceived us. It had nothing to do with Jesus Christ except the enemy wanting to blind us from Him with unhealthy entertainment.

We look nothing like a Frankenstein. The mad scientist was so obsessed with creating a human being that only he could bring to life and show the world his creation. You can imagine what Hollywood was thinking and feeling after this became one of biggest movies ever in the 50's, 60's and 70's (that I knew of). Every household that had a television knew about Frankenstein.

A few things about Frankenstein: First, he was not created nor revived by God. Secondly, He was not created to show love nor walk in God's image. Only man is created in God's image and likeness. Nothing else was created in God's image. Frankenstein was a product of a mad scientist who wanted to gain worldwide fame in the scientific community and to show the world his achievement. There always had to be a victim's body that the mad scientist used. It would either be from a grave site or through committing a murder. Isn't that just like the devil who wants to use your body and make you his puppet? Sadly, there are so many people that allow the devil to use them like puppets under his control. Those kinds of people desperately need to surrender their lives to Jesus, right now. The problem went even further in society, a few years ago, when scientists wanted to start cloning human beings. People have issues with power and wanting to be in control of what God is already in control of. The test was with dolly the sheep.

What is much more important to us is that Holy Spirit wants to remind us of who our Creator is, and He wants to use our vessels (body), talents and gifts for love and His glory. Don't allow the enemy to use you like you are his Frankenstein. Ask God to fill you with the Holy Spirit (Ephesians 5:18) so His power can manifest in your life to give Him glory!

Another movie people flocked to see was "Dracula". This kind of movie was severely evil and could easily take over your spirit if you have not accepted Jesus Christ as Lord and Savior. The Dracula movie was always centered on his vicious teeth biting a women's neck. Then she became a vampire and/or his bride. The point is that the devil wants to take a bite out you today! This show as I understand today was a direct attack on our culture. Saints turn your television off or to another station with something peaceable and wholesome, especially inside your children's room. Give them the gospel to read instead of watching evil movies that may allow spirits to come through the television. They may seem harmless until you start having nightmares that seem so real. Jesus wants you to accept His spirit to come inside your heart which is far greater and powerful than any of those evil movie characters. Don't let the enemy take a bite out of your mind, spirit, soul nor body. Let Jesus enter your heart because of His love for you. Jesus makes so many things so easy! Stepping into the Kingdom as a new Kingdom child is powerful yet pleasing in God's sight. God wants His people to experience a paradise filled with blessings as in the beginning with Adam and Eve.

Love was poured inside of us when God formed us. Therefore, we were created for love. God never makes a mistake. God's people will never be a product of a Frankenstein scientist experiment. His people will always be children of God (Galatians 3:26; John 1:12; Romans 8:14, Hebrews 2:14). It will not change. We belong to the one God that formed us from the ground. Our primary purpose in life is to worship and serve our Lord, Jesus. God reveals the power of love through Jesus death on the cross and resurrection. He is the only one that can max-out on love. Jesus was the Lamb of God who took away the sin of the world. Stop taking this statement for granted. Instead give God praise and glory at the thought of His love for you.

Love is revealed through the marriage union which was established by God. Most importantly, God is love and whatever He created and ordained he did it out of His love for His people. When He created man in his likeness and image, it was because God wanted man to walk in the love of Jesus Christ. No other created being has this capacity. He designed and desires that man walk in His image. We are to mirror the character of Jesus Christ. We need to understand clearly that when God breathed in man's nostril the breath of life, man became a living soul (creature). He became a living being to live for God's purpose. The breath of life is the breath of love from God to man. We are to live in the deepness of love. The breath of life was love going throughout Adam's entire body and spiritual makeup. Love was present. He created Man to have a life in paradise. He already gave man his destiny in the beginning when He created him. God infused His love inside of man's heart and his spirit, so we can walk in the image of God. Adam was not a test. Adam was reality to what God created for His purpose of manifesting life, love, power for His glorification and use. He created man to love and be his servants of our Lord, God. We were created to love. The opposition is a fallen angel named Satan whom we recognize as the devil. God sent him to hell. He came on the scene after displaying pride in heaven and God cast him out of heaven to hell. Nevertheless, Adam's other issue was in his house. GENESIS 3:6-7 When the woman saw that the fruit of the tree was good for food and pleasing to the eye, and also desirable for gaining wisdom, she took some and ate it. She also gave some to her husband, who was with her, and he ate it. Then the eyes of both were opened, and they realized they were naked; so, they sewed fig leaves together and made coverings for themselves. Disobedience and rebellion are the issues against God! You see if we love God, we will walk in obedience.

God gave man the freedom to choose. We have a free choice to live in obedience to God. We always have the upper hand because we belong to God. We were made to love because God is love. Love has power. Nevertheless, we were also created to acknowledge to God that we love Him and will obey. Man was lost when he chose to partake of the fruit presented by Satan. Please remember that Adam had the authority to run the devil out and cause his wife to put the fruit down. He failed at making the right choice and became disobedient to God. Prove to God that you love Him, today. Show Him that you will become a God Runner and help save souls to the glory of the Father.

JESUS COMMMANDS US TO LOVE!

WE WERE CREATED TO OBEY GOD'S COMMANDS

Matthew 22: 37-39 Jesus said unto him, Thou shalt love the Lord thy God with all thy heart, and with all thy soul, and with all thy mind. This is the first and great commandment. And the second is like unto it, Thou shalt love thy neighbor as thyself.

It is extremely important to always make sure to buckle up on any road before taking off. Your seatbelt will save your life! When you get on any of these interstates anything can happen. Sudden lane switching happens all day long on the road and interstates and the unexpected can easily occur as well. Life insurance is a must! Nevertheless, you need to pray before driving anywhere. Things have changed drastically with people's attitudes, behavior and lack of courtesy. As a Christian, be better than others in behavior and attitude. Pray for safety for everyone.

Some people say that I 278 and 268 in New York, the Turn Pike in New Jersey, I 5 N San Diego, US Highway 101 in Hollywood, California are the most dangerous highways. Now you know to pray before driving. You don't know the next person's move no matter how good of a driver you are! Occasionally, I have caught myself driving off and putting on my seat belt at the same time. It should be buckled, before 3we drive off. I should be secure in case someone in another vehicle loses control. No excuse!

I've thought about the laws on the road and the state troopers enforcing them. Now I am beginning to see it as an act of love when people get stopped for speeding, under the influence of alcohol or drugs, talking on a cell phone, changing lanes excessively and just flat out speeding. Police should act, instead of letting it go without a warning at the minimum. Many people have been guilty and always want to be excused and given a second chance. Some acts warrant a second chance, and some do not! Law enforcement should stop drivers before they crash and kill innocent people. Some have killed entire families because of careless and selfishness behavior on the cell phone. Police officers give out tickets to save someone else's life. In the movie "Seven Pounds" by Will Smith, the driver was on the cell phone and took his eyes off the road then lost control flipping the vehicle, crashing it resulting in killing his wife as she was thrown from the vehicle. In that movie, the pain was so deep that it never left him until he took his own life to donate his body parts to people in need.

Do not follow his example! Don't take your life over a mistake! God forgives you and loves you! Surrender your life to God! The actor had so much compassion in his heart to give back what he had taken from one life. Don't get to that point in your life when it's too late. Do not allow a selfish lifestyle to cause you to do something so hurtful to someone else and yourself. Love is when you stop speeding, drinking, and driving and talking on the cell phone selfishly while driving on any street, road, or highway. I saw one lady so mad on the phone while driving it was scary! Another important part of driving is speed. The speed limit is much like a commandment but it's from the law enforcement agency. Love is demonstrated when you stop speeding on the highway and prepare your vehicle with all safety measures. Big trucks need proper tarps! People with trailers should not have any lose objects like small bricks or boards unsecured. Please secure it. One man was driving with three lose bricks that was waiting to bounce out and hit a windshield and kill an entire family because he did not take time. God wants you to slow it down on the highway. Prove to God that you love Him by obeying Him.

Love is displayed in so many ways because we were created to love. Another thing that comes to mind is the intensity of love and joy that marriage and family brings. More importantly, making vows before Jesus is a promise that should not be broken because God takes it seriously! If you start out taking your vows lightly, you may have extreme issues in your marriage. Make no mistake about it; God wants your heart and obedience first. In fact, the primary way of illustrating your love for Jesus is your obedience and receiving Him in your heart. He wants you to completely love Him back and prove it to Him! Surrender your heart to him and you will obey the Lord without pressure. Surrender your heart today and you will encounter blessings in abundance!

One example of love displayed is when we see couples holding each other's hands in the park and kissing. Another view of love is when a man and woman are getting married. Jesus must be the center of your marriage from day one until death do you part.

You can also observe love during family reunions. Love is also displayed when you see people providing and coming together for others who experienced a natural disaster like a level-5 tornado or a flood.

The command to love is not a one-time thing, then you're done. You can't turn love off like a light switch. The enemy is always trying to divide the house by stirring up confusion, disagreements, and offenses. The enemy is targeting you, so don't be surprised. Keep your guard up. Another display of love is when a person bends over backwards to help another person. This kind of love entails helping someone living on the street or in a bad financial situation or some other circumstance. Nevertheless, it is still a display of love. We are not to have the same attitudes of that like the Levite and the priest displayed when they passed by the broken man. They walked by the man who was beaten badly; but the Samaritan man fixed Him up and paid for his room (Luke 10:25-37). The Good Samaritan displayed what I call bending over backwards and going the extra distance for someone you don't even know. The Good Samaritan did it! Why can't you? We should be that kind of neighbor. Pray and ask Jesus for a gentle heart to love God and your neighbor. It is easy if you allow the Holy Spirit to take over. Tell the evil spirit and flesh to move out! Let the King of Glory come inside you.

Jesus went beyond bending over backwards. In fact, that is an understatement because nothing can compare to Jesus dying on the cross. When you read the miracles that Jesus performed in the Bible, that is enough to captivate our minds forever. He healed men with leprosy. He healed a man under the authority of a centurion Soldier. He healed a man with a withered hand. He healed a blind man (John 9).

Jesus commands us to love. Jesus is speaking to us in this command so that we will prioritize our love, making him first in our heart, soul, spirit, and mind. This is the first and greatest command according to Jesus (Matthew 22). Love is the highest priority in life because without it, humanity would not survive. Trouble, hatred, and evil would rule the world. Love has God's power in it. Jesus wants to know that you will give your life to Him and fall in love with Him. I thought about King David. Once he realized the greatness and goodness of God, He opened and danced before God naked. He realized that he could give himself totally to God. He not only did that act of worship, he wrote the Psalms that specifically give praise to God. He is so good! You will know when someone want to max out in loving God is when they worship, praise him, love God with all thine heart, mind, and soul. This is a person who commits to God on a high level in life with humility and reverence. Another person that comes to my mind is Noah. Of course, Noah found grace in the eyes of God. He was obedient in constructing an ark because God instructed him to save his house and set an example of listening to the voice of God. The ark represents a covering of love, family, and commitment. I would also have to mention Elijah who followed God and depended on God's power in a showdown with Baal, Jezebel's idols, and false prophets.

Questions & Discussion:

1. What does the command to love mean? _____

2. Who gave the command to love and why? _____

3. Have you obeyed this command in Matthew 22? If, so When?
_____
_____

4. What steps do you plan to take to obey the command in Matthew 22?
_____
_____

5. List five scripture that can help you with obeying this command._____
_____
_____

6. List 2 incidents in which you found it difficult to obey the command and how you overcame it.
_____
_____
_____
_____

CHAPTER 3

THE LOVE COMPASS

Two huge things come to my mind when I hear the words love compass. My first thought is finding direction to the source of love. People always will need directions and confirmation. One main intent is that you find your way back to God if you fell away! The power of love will lead you back to the Lord, our God. In the spiritual world that means finding Jesus and accepting Him as Lord and Savior.

Today, we have the Holy Spirit as our compass to guide us (John 16), if Jesus is our Lord and Savior. The land navigation compass and map reveal the true north and grid north. Those two are very helpful, however, the one who controls all norths is God. Every Christian has this advantage. The Holy Spirit guides those that belong to him. You should ask Jesus to come into your heart if you do not have a relationship with him! (Romans 10:9)

My second thought took me back to joining the military and being able to make it through basic training. Using a compass is one requirement, as well as using a map to get through the land navigation course. You must know how to follow direction to pass the test. You should also know where you are located always.

I also thought about the Titanic moving under a false, misguided or inoperable navigation system and no one at the controls. Although it was a huge luxury liner on the vast ocean, it still needed to use an instrument for navigation, as well as someone at the control center to guide it. Because the compass (navigation system) was not constantly observed nor used properly, the ship ran into an iceberg and sunk to the bottom of the ocean. The worst of it was that thousands of lives were lost because of an unmonitored navigation system. The Captain was not at the controls. Can you imagine how the captain of that ship felt in his heart when he discovered what happened?

Likewise, 747 Jet liners also need to have state of the art navigation systems (a compass) and competent pilots to get customers to the right location through the air. If that compass and GPS is broken, the pilot can easily take the wrong direction and crash into another plane or mountain, God forbid! It's a good thing that Jesus is on your flight to save your life twice!

In the Armed Forces, each soldier is required to complete a land navigation course and exam. You must know how to read the map and compass. After all, you are a soldier and if you have no sense of direction, you will be lost more than once. If you have no sense of direction, you can't lead soldiers not to mention a wife. If you have no sense of direction, you can't even lead a church as a pastor. The love compass can lead you anywhere at any time.

My unit commander chose their elite soldier to participate in a challenge call the "Night Riders Course". On or around 10 October 1991 while stationed in Germany, I had to represent my unit in maneuvering over vast terrain during (absolute darkness) where we had to drive in blackout drive (no bright lights on). When you are in that kind of situation your senses kick in overdrive. At that time, I was thinking, during that night land navigation test, I had to put all the terrain in my mind from the map and visualize roads and turning point as well as short cuts with no light. My mind had to think with confidence where I was going. I needed that compass to orient myself before I took off in the vehicle. I found every point faster than I thought I would, as we moved fast in our Humvee. I passed every test event at each stopping point with a "GO." Can you imagine how I felt after achieving this? I felt highly confident and that God loved me and kept me as He guided me through all the points and back home. The compass had to be used at the beginning for sure.

The Holy Spirit must always be used all the way through life as our compass. For those who do not know Jesus, He wants to be your love compass. Jesus opens His arms daily for you to come to Him.

Today you need to find your way to understand the power of love and where it's truly located. The power of love is in Jesus Christ, our Lord and Savior. You can view the movie "The Passion of Christ" and you will not need any further advice. This love in Jesus Christ is the only true love! Jesus Christ is the core foundation and the very existence of love. It is from Jesus Christ, we draw the love we have inside of us. The foundation of love inside of us is from God. To find the love you desire, use the love compass that you were given. There is power in having a regular compass. Its primary use is for direction, staying on path and finding the source and destination point. Jesus is our destination point and source. We also need to understand that the Holy Spirit gives us directions for living the Christian life! He does not give directions to just live any old life. God created us to follow His way of love. He gave us the Holy Spirit of promise (John16)! God gave us His best, Jesus Christ! God created us to walk with Jesus and be led in the Spirit. Therefore, He has revealed to us the compass for love. Jesus Christ, the Son of the living God is our compass and source for love and life itself (John 3:16). Jesus is our light in the darkness, without Him, we would be lost. It was Jesus Christ, my Lord that helped me through that Night Rider Course in Germany in 1991. In Psalm 119:105 the Bible says, "You are a lamp for my feet, a light on my path" Think about it! If there is no Jesus, we are lost because He is our light! Think harder about it! He has given us the Holy Spirit to be the light and compass for the rest of our lives. He gives us directions in true love from God. His love is straight forward, and at the same time powerful and mysterious. His love is unlimited! His love will never let you get lost, when you accept Him as Lord and Savior. His love is expressed in His Word. His love is our compass for life! It does not matter what course we are on if we are believers, He will guide us back to Himself with the power of love.

Jesus reveals His love every day in our lives. If you are a believer, the love of God is never absent in your life. You always have the power of love walking with you. Even when the enemy attacks and you make a mistake, God takes you right back under His love and care. In fact, He never leaves you. The Bible is clear in Hebrews 13:5 "Let your conversation be without covetousness; and be content with such things as ye have: for he hath said, I will never leave thee, nor forsake thee." God keeps His word that He will remain with you to help you in life. When you realize this, you will exalt His name because of who He is and what He has done in your life. If you are a nonbeliever, Jesus is still caring for you! If He did not, you would not be alive. Even when you ignore Him, shut Him out, act like He is not real, Jesus is still pouring out love in your life. He still wants you to crossover into the Kingdom of God. Some ignore Him because they take God for granted. God wants you to search your heart. This book is to enlighten you and direct you to your Bible, which is the word of God, so you will be transformed and become committed to God. You commit to God because of His love for you and because He is the one that pours out blessings in your life daily. You should thank Him daily! The love compass is to help draw you and direct you to the word of God and change your life. You may not be living for Jesus right now. Nevertheless, at the end of this reading, I pray you will be convinced that your life must be turned over to Jesus.

The love compass is a book. These writings are influenced by the word of God, Matthew 22:37-39 "Love the Lord your God with all your heart and with all your soul and with your entire mind. This is the first and greatest commandment. And the second is like it: 'Love your neighbor as yourself."

First, what is a compass? It is an instrument used for directions like in the military for soldiers to find and plot directions. A compass is also used on vessels such as huge cruise liners, army, navy and marine ships in navigating huge bodies of water. If a large or small ship on the ocean does not have its compass in operation, it can easily drift off course. Most people remember the Titanic and the cost paid for drifting off course. That ship lost thousands of people. They died because the ship sank and there weren't enough lifeboats. Those sent to rescue the passengers from the ocean's cold water were not available in time.

However, Jesus give us this compass in Matthew 16:18-25 as well in so many other scripture verses. Use the word of God as a compass to navigate your life. We need to have the anointing of love on us to take the right direction. The enemy comes to kill, steal, and destroy. Jesus comes to give life and give it more abundantly. I love this because He does not put an age limit on this.

An ordinary compass points in four directions (North, South, East, and West) but God's love compass covers all areas beyond those four directions. You can use the love compass regardless of where you are standing. God's love has no limits. God loves is so powerful that it can penetrate death and snatch His Saints (1 Thessalonian 4). But there is a problem for those who reject Him. Their destination is hell (Luke 16). Jesus has defeated the devil, hell, and the grave. Therefore, love conquers all things. I want you to see that this compass point is available for all people. Make your first stop to worship and exalt His name. Thank him for His love! The compass of Matthew 22:37 and John 3:16 are to prove to you that Jesus' love is unlimited. The compass wants to direct you to someone you hate, dislike, or hold a grudge against. Love is so powerful that it digs deep into the soul of man. Love is so powerful that it forgives. Love settles arguments and diminishes strife. Love overpowers all enemy attacks. The next time you get attacked, call on Jesus for love. Say Lord, Jesus, please send the power of love in this situation. Love has the power to break through bad thoughts even when PTSD is present in a soldier's mind. Love settles it and gets rid of it. The more the love of Jesus is demonstrated in your life, the more you get all the bad stuff out of your system and your life. Keep love as the central power of your life. In so many cases, people need to find their way back to love. God is the love compass. Only God our Lord can change an evil person into a loving and caring person.

Have you ever stopped at a gas station to refuel your car or truck? It costs around $30-$60. God does not charge us to refuel your body with His love. In fact, He not only refuels us, He infuses us with His love, so we will never run out. If you are a child of God you never see empty, you only operate on full. Therefore, you can love God back. Ask Jesus for directions with your love compass that He put in you. You will never be lost! Your love compass points to Jesus. So, keep holding your compass toward heaven and watch your needle. It will have a heavenly magnetic pull for everyone to see.

Questions & Discussion:

1. What is the love compass to you?
_____
_____

2. Where do you think the needle will point on your compass for love?
_____
_____

3. Name other locations that you want the compass needle to point to?
_____
_____

4. How would you use the love compass for relationships?
_____
_____

CHAPTER 4

THE ANOINTED ONE

1 Samuel 16:12-13 And he sent, and brought him in. Now he was ruddy, and withal of a beautiful countenance, and goodly to look to. And the Lord said, Arise, anoint him: for this is he. Then Samuel took the horn of oil, and anointed him in the midst of his brethren: and the Spirit of the Lord came upon David from that day forward. So Samuel rose up, and went to Ramah.

I first want to say that Jesus was anointed to love all people. He came to save and anoint people to be His disciples (or followers). He is God in the flesh! He demonstrated it in spirit and in bodily form. He was anointed for the mission for which He was assigned; saving people from their sins. One of the most important words in the Bible that is overlooked or under emphasized when we think of Jesus is the word Christ. Most people do not even know that the word Christ means anointed one or chosen one. The word Christ is derived from the Greek word Christos (khris-tos) which means anointed or anointed one. Christ is also a translation of the Hebrew word Messiah (mashiach). So, when you hear those two words Christ or Messiah, it simply means the anointed one. Every Christian needs to know what this means. Obviously "Christ" is part of the word Christian. I am mentioning this word because when you look at it, you can identify that Jesus' followers are supposed to be anointed as well, since Jesus dwells inside your heart in spirit. We are to walk and claim our membership in the family of God as Christian and believers. You are supposed to be anointed for missions as followers of Jesus Christ. We are givers in the Kingdom and for the Kingdom because Jesus constantly gave to the world and anyone who needed Him! Nevertheless, Jesus was anointed not just for His mission to give His life on the cross for the world; it was to prove that He is Lord of Lords and King of Kings. Jesus was anointed because His Father anointed Him. In the Biblical times, to be anointed was the act of having sacred oil poured on one's head and to be recognized as set apart for God's use. Are you set apart for God? You will see this happening with the Prophet Samuel when he anoints King David in 1 Samuel 16. This kind of anointing with oil was used for priests, kings, and prophets. The anointing is a special blessing and used on people set apart for God's use in ministry. You can't put oil on people because you want to, or to feel so holy and sanctified. Oil is placed on a person's head to anoint and set them apart for God's use and influence. This should not be under man's direction or influence. It needs to be under the Holy Spirit's influence. A person should be led by Jesus Christ. God must select the person to be anointed. In another view of the anointing, King David also saw the importance of not touching God's anointed (1 Samuel 24:6). He had the right reverent attitude because when God anoints a man of God, everyone's hands, mouth and tongue must be off the man of God. Even in the story of Elisha, God's anointed man of God, there were some little boys who were making fun of Elisha, God saw it and unleased two female bears that ripped 42 boys apart (2 Kings 2:23-25). Keep your mouth and heart off the Man of God. Touch not mine anointed and do my prophet no harm (1 Chronicles 16:22). You might not see it now, but if you did something, please go into deep repentance because God's word does not fail. He forgives a repentant heart.

    I also believe when God mentions His five-fold ministry in (Ephesians 4:11) they also are also recognized by God as anointed people selected by God to serve His people. Therefore, to be anointed means that God has selected or chosen you for specific tasks. For these selected, to anoint also means to smear or rub oil on a specific person in a religious ceremony for God's purpose. The origin of anoint comes from shepherds used oil on sheep to keep lice and other insects from getting into the ears of sheep and killing them.

When God ordains a chosen person, He sets them apart for a special mission in ministry. The person chosen has special holy orders to carry out for the Lord. No one gets ordained to just sit in church and look holy and special. As an ordained minister, you must be activated to win souls. Jesus' special task was to die on a cross for the sin of the world and rise from the grave defeating death, grave, the devil and sin. Jesus's anointing was from God, the Father. He was anointed to show the power of love, grace, truth, mercy, miracles, and super natural power from God our Father in Heaven. Even in the beginning in Genesis 49:10 Jacob blessed his son and foretold of this great King, our Lord. Another clear prophecy regarding our future messianic King is directed from the fact that God had established David's family line after him. God made it clear that from David's family a King would come, and this King's Kingdom would have no end (1 Chronicles 17:11-14). It is also important to know that Matthew 2 was the fulfillment of Psalm 72 and Isaiah 60. The anointing was present at Jesus's birth. We know it because an angel of the Lord (Gabriel) announced to Mary (Luke 1:26-38). We know because several kings saw a special star in the east and the kings recognized its significance and travelled to honor the new King of the world (Matthew 2). Jesus was the anointed one to express the greatest of God's love from birth to death and resurrection. Jesus was anointed specifically to point everyone to His Father in Heaven (Luke 4). He bridged the gap that no one else could. His resurrection is the power of love and life in Jesus Christ. God was showing all of us that we also are to walk in newness of life as though we are resurrected from our old lives to a new life in Jesus Christ (Romans 6). We serve the living God and His son Jesus Christ who is at the right hand of the Father in heaven.

Questions:

1. Who anointed David in 1 Samuel 16?_____

2. Who did God anoint for sinner? _____

CHAPTER 5

PERFECT LOVE

1 John 4:16-18 And we have known and believed the love that God hath to us. God is love; and he that dwelleth in love dwelleth in God, and God in him. Herein is our love made perfect, that we may have boldness in the day of judgment: because as he is, so are we in this world. There is no fear in love; but perfect love casteth out fear: because fear hath torment. He that feareth is not made perfect in love.

There are relationships where men and women believe that the one they love is perfect and/or flawless. Love has an effect on everyone especially if its true love. A situation like this, can lead to a fear of this person leaving for another person. God wants us to know Him and stop breaking His heart! He also wants us to depend on His love! We, as Christians, believe by faith that perfect love is in Him only. We believe that He cast out any fear because His love is perfected in us. We must realize that love is also considered on the Day of Judgment. Therefore, love God with all your heart!

Perfect love casts out fear. Perfect love is flawless, error free and has complete and perfect power from Jesus Christ. Perfect love is the answer to troubles and hardened hearts. Perfect love gives you confidence to know to whom you belong. You don't have to worry about being judged. The word perfect in Webster is defined as freedom from fault and defect. Another definition is an exemplification of supreme excellence. The love of God that dwells in you is more powerful than any kind of fear. What is fear? Fear is an emotion that can easily take you over and make you feel like danger is imminent. Fear sends signals to the brain to make you respond from a protective posture and causes you to be alert. Fear in some cases might help in a survival situation. Other kinds of fear aren't helpful, such as fear of losing something or someone, fear of pain, or a medical diagnosis or procedures, fear of the unknown (not knowing fact or your future), fear of not having control over your life, fear of not being liked or popular, etc. Most fear has something to do with the enemy deceiving you. Much of fear is associated with punishment and/or lack of control or your life. It can stem from evil attacks, regardless if you are a believer or not. You have a better chance at overcoming it as a believer in Jesus Christ. We also know that for most teenage girls and boys, they have a strong fear of rejection. To combat this fear, receive the love of Jesus inside your heart. Fear is a weapon from the devil-Satan. God sets us free from all fear! Fear is also present when you desire someone, but they do not return your love. God is telling you to value yourself and move on to something better! Did you get that? There is something better for you in the future at the right time!

Nevertheless, the Apostle John wants us to know that love has power over torment which is also associated with fear. In fact, we can easily see fear as a torment in our lives. Think about it, stress is one of the leading causes of strokes and heart attack which leads to death. You can deal with stress by letting it go in Jesus Christ through prayer. You can also exercise and eat healthy and put your mind on things pure, happy and fun with laughter! Ask Jesus to allow love to dwell in your heart, mind, soul, and spirit. (Matthew 22:36-37). You need a solid relationship with Jesus Christ (Romans 10:9) so ask Him to come into your heart right now. When He enters your heart, you have the power of love on your side. Love can cast out all the negative things of the enemy. The spirit of fear is defeated in Jesus Christ. If you are God's children, fear can't have a hold on you, nor will it control you. You need to activate your faith in Jesus Christ to get over any fear. You have the King of Kings inside of your heart. The Father, Son and Holy Spirit have perfect love that dominates all fear. You see love has so much power that it dominates anything against you. Love is every part of your life and in Jesus Christ. When you get a taste of perfect love, you can have an almost perfect relationship as a married couple.

Questions & Discussion:

1. What is said about love in this scripture 1 John 4:16-18?

_____
_____
_____

2. List three people in the Bible that experienced perfect love.

_____
_____
_____

3. What kind of fear does perfect love cast out in people lives?

_____
_____

4. How can perfect love restore your life?

_____
_____
_____

CHAPTER 6

POSITIONED TO LOVE

People think of positions in various ways. A position is defined as a place in which someone has put something in a specific way. One example of a position is in the world of employment. Economists are always discussing economic growth in the job markets. Many government leaders prize their efforts in trying to create jobs. Each person that desires to work spends time and effort to develop that resume for the perfect position. Making money and having a sense of belonging and self-worth means something. When that specific job comes available, it's time to position one's self to shine before those conducting the interview. I was working a temporary job in the college. Because I did not desire to remain in that position, I kept on looking for a better job. I landed a job working in the military with soldiers who were returning from war wounded and broken. I finally found where I needed to be from God's view point. I knew it by observing the wounded soldiers and listening to the Lord's voice. It was confirmed that a ministry had to be birth through me from this job position. God has caused it to be a launching pad ministry. More fruit is being processes for the glory of God.

Men and women can be extremely powerful when they get into the right position to share God's word to those lost in the world. The Lord simply spoke to me that nothing was stopping me! All I had to do was be obedient and step out in faith and serve!

God expects us to answer and start serving. Saints you need to be in a position where God can use you according to His purpose. Listen, be in position and the right place to receive the word before you share it. Sharing the word of God is one of the most powerful things you can do! The word of God has the power to change things. However, you need to position yourself to be an effective witness. Your potential is unlimited in Jesus Christ.

Saints, we get into position simply by repenting of our sin (1 John 1:9) and trusting God to use us as an instrument (witness) to save souls. You get into position by receiving Jesus inside of your heart (Romans 10:9-10). You get into position by learning and sharing God's word with someone you know is down and out! The most critical assignment to each man and woman is their own household! At times, it may be more beneficial to give small nuggets to those who live with you. For example, give one or two small scriptures such as Isaiah 54:10 where He tells us that "His unfailing love for us will never be shaken." Later dive into some scriptural stories like, Joseph's dream and his coming out of the pit and becoming the second highest leader in the world after Pharaoh! (Genesis 37:23-28).

Moses was also in the right position and at the right time for God to intervene in his life to be used by God. Moses positioned himself before a burning bush in which God spoke to him. From that position, God perhaps gave him one of the biggest mission in the Bible which was to tell Pharaoh to "let my people go (Exodus 9:1)." Because God said it, it had to come to pass.

If God has given you the ministry and directions to witness to other people, then God himself will position you for his glory and purpose. God is the God of blessings. You can also tell your family that He is the God from everlasting to everlasting (Psalms 90). Tell them Jesus is the God that changes situations that no one else can change. Tell then that the Holy Spirit will give them guidance (John 16).

You can't just run and hide. You have to get into position to let people know that you bear fruit for the King of Glory. Let them know you are a Kingdom Child of the Most High! You are in position because you are sanctified in Jesus Christ. You can also share a testimony as to what He did in your life.

The Lord wants every man and woman to get in position to receive more of his love daily. Our biggest problem is that we get out of position. We put ourselves in positions for other things that are not Godly. Some people almost break their necks to please other people who know nothing about you. The Lord is telling you, me, and others to get into position to receive the power of his love that will work through you. Why position yourself? You position yourself, so you can be an overcomer. We position ourselves to receive the power of love that overflows and make us better people. We position ourselves to overcome loses, pain, break ups, and heartaches. We position ourselves to become more obedient and walk in the blessings of God.

Love has the power to bring families together; and dismiss all fear, pain, hate, and negative behavior and attitudes that have been blocking family relationships. We need love. God supplies it and never lets us down. People around us will let us down because they don't know us, or they may not have the love of Jesus. God has placed people in your life to encourage you, but remember, people are not perfect. Jesus reveals His perfected love to us daily. We, as people, can do our best. However, we need to count on Jesus. His love overflows. There is power in His name! Hallelujah Jesus' love will comfort you. This is your day to position yourself. Every woman position yourself to receive God's love. Every man, son, and daughter. Mark this day and remember Jesus is changing your life forever. You will never go without love again.

It is the power of love that positions us and affects us in every area of life. We strive to position ourselves to reach that level of restoration in our marriages and families. Three of the most critical areas in relationships are each person's love language and expression which aids in positive and clear communication. It can affect your behavior in the marriage. How do you behave in your marriage? Do you make the marriage difficult? How do you communicate in your marriage? How do you express your love to your spouse? Do you ever check your heart? Are you submissive to your husband? Is there romance in the marriage?

Is there manipulation in your marriage? Are you a woman with a controlling spirit? I have seen several women like that being overbearing to their husbands in public and belittling him. In fact, many marriages have one of the spouses operating in a controlling spirit. It can be either the wife or the husband with the controlling spirit. The adversary attacks at husbands perhaps more frequently. The enemy wants to control both of you to destroy your relationship.

We as men and women need to get into position for a breakthrough and blessings in our marriage. The position of the wife is to become the helpmate that God made her. This is an extremely critical component and purpose to operate in. If she never positions herself as God properly as a helpmeet, then the marriage will experience turbulence and possible tragedy! Don't let the devil get a foothold in your marriage. He will attack the woman to get at the husband. If she positions herself as a wife and helpmeet, the marriage will be a Godly and successful one (Genesis 2:18). Her role in his life is a divine and powerful one that is God centered. It should be approached with the utmost importance. If you allow something to break this relationship, you may not have been truly the right connection. You need to make sure that you are equally yoked to survive marriage. Both of you need to be Christians and Jesus must be in the marriage. Look below at what a help meet means.

According to (Dobson et al., 1994) when referring to help meet, the Hebrew word is Ezer which means simply in English, help. The word means to rescue and save. I know every man wants to hear this meaning. Can you imagine a brother asking his wife to save me? As men, we can see now why God gave us a woman. She is more than a gift. God told Adam what Eve was to him. She was created to save her husband throughout life. In 1 Samuel 7:12 another word is used which is Ebenezer and Eben haezer which means according to Adam Clarke commentary, "The Stone of Help;" perhaps a pillar is meant by the word stone (Adam Clarke commentary, 1832). 1 Samuel 7:12 says "Then Samuel took a stone and set it between Mizpah and Shen, and named it Ebenezer, saying, "Thus far the LORD has helped us" (Adam Clarke commentary, 1832). I believe this is powerful because the women not only support, but she constantly helps him to be successful in the Lord Jesus Christ. In so many ways, she is his minster and He is her priest and covering. Then God is the joining factor. Many people might view this as women being motivated to help bring their husband to our Lord Jesus! In a sense she helps to deliver her husband to God to be born again. The woman is positioned to save her husband and household. One of the major points in this entire summary is that God shows love in such a powerful way to maximize it in relationship with Him and the marriage.

GET INTO THE RIGHT PLACE AND POSITION

(TO TESTIFY!)

This morning, I was going to take the day off because there was repetition in my mind saying, you are too tired to go to work! Stay home! No one will miss you. It's time for you to retire and do nothing! You have already reached retirement at your job if you choose to take it. I was almost convinced to stay home. I received help in the form of my wife texting me a honey-do list. I know the help really came from the Holy Spirit. I got excited if you know what I mean! It pushed me right out the door! You can figure that out! Why would I stay home to do all that work? She is so creative, and the list will never end! Trust me, I work for her. Nevertheless, I went in to my job and worked for my pay check. I realized that God gave me a job over thousands of people. The other form of help was through the Holy Spirit closing the mouth of that adversary, so I could not listen to his voice. I also had to tell myself that I am not defeated! I had to speak words of encouragement to myself and believe in God, my Lord in Jesus name! I am not tired! I had to rebuke that voice that was trying to get into my head! I told myself that I am strong in the Lord and in the power of His might! I spoke the word of God "Greater is He in me than he in the world (John 4)." I heard the Holy Spirit telling me to serve Him with all my heart. The Holy Spirit reminded me just as Jesus told Peter, if you love me, feed my sheep (John 21:7), which really means show me your dedication! It also means preach the word and be a servant to God. Be instant in season and out of season (2 Timothy 4:2)! Humble yourself before the

Lord, and he will lift you up (James 4:10)! You must be in position to receive it and activate your faith to get results!

The Holy Spirit reminded me that I am blessed in every way (Deuteronomy 28)! Read it and believe it! The Holy Spirit also reminded me that He gave me this job for a reason. He allowed me to have this job working with wounded warriors from combat operations. He spoke to me, as plain as day, "Go and launch a ministry in Jesus name for exalting Him, and serving, healing, and restoring the lives of lost and wounded soldiers and their families! God said go and get into position to witness with His word! Preach and deliver it now! The Holy Spirit said to me that you will obey. Matthew 28:18-20 says "Go baptize in the name of the Father, Son and Holy Ghost." I stepped into a pastoral position under the influence of the Holy Spirit and have been serving God for over nine years. People are getting baptized, families are being restored and people are looking to serve God in the church and outside the walls! This little ministry is bigger than its numbers because God is in it. It's already more than a mega ministry because you can't put a number on God! The Holy Spirit teaches and draws willing souls! The Holy Spirit is truth and has the power to persuade you to love God back (John 16:3-13)! As soon as I obeyed God and went to work, I had an office with three people waiting to ask me questions about Jesus. One woman wanted to get her children dedicated to the Lord. Another person wanted their home dedicated! Another person wanted their family baptized. I go to work and people are waiting for the move of God and some of them, I have never met!

As soon as I got into my office at work, a high-ranking soldier, Lieutenant Colonel (LTC) was waiting and entered my office for in-processing. As he was asking me questions for training, he noticed church cards on my desk which reveals scripture and my position in the church as the Pastor. He was led to ask me questions about being born again (Romans 10:9), (John 3:3) and baptism. I closed my door and took him to (Romans 10:9) and (Romans 6:1-10) so he could see the power associated with the resurrection of Jesus Christ when we get baptized. I also showed him the empowerment of the spiritual baptism of fire in Act 1:8 and Act 2. This LTC had all kinds of knowledge to lead and strategize with soldiers in preparation for military missions, but he knew nothing about salvation and being empowered by the Holy Spirit to serve God. He asked Jesus to come into his heart and now he is born again. Today He knows and acknowledges Jesus as Lord and Savior. Get into position to love by sharing Jesus with others at a moment's notice. Start thinking about the different positions you can be in to share the word of God and win a soul to Jesus Christ. Some places to position yourself to share the word of God is the grocery store, mall shopping center, department stores, the Military base, in your office, break rooms, in the church parking lot, inside the church, sometimes you can share while in the car transporting.

Questions & Discussion:

1. Why would God want you to be in position for love?
_____
_____
_____

2. How do you get in position? List three things.
_____
_____

_____

3. What does John 3:3 and Romans 6:1-10 mean to you?
_____

4. What does Acts 1:8 and Act 2 mean to you?
_____
_____

5. What does James 4:10 mean? _____

CHAPTER 7

THE MIRACLE MAKER

John 2:1-6 And the third day there was a marriage in Cana of Galilee; and the mother of Jesus was there: And both Jesus was called, and his disciples, to the marriage. And when they wanted wine, the mother of Jesus saith unto him, They have no wine. Jesus saith unto her, Woman, what have I to do with thee? mine hour is not yet come. His mother saith unto the servants, Whatsoever he saith unto you, do it. And there were set there six waterpots of stone, after the manner of the purifying of the Jews, containing two or three firkins apiece.

Love is God's character and identity! Love flows from God to each person's life. Everything good stems from God! His miracles stem from the power of His love. His death on the cross and the resurrection were the ultimate acts of God's love for all creation. Miracles reveal the power of God's love. Every act of rescuing people and demonstrating miracles in their lives come from God! Angels are in position to be dispatched by God to spread love, joy and peace in the world among all families of the earth. God's love is shown even in the animal kingdom. He provides pets for us to bring out the best in us.

Jesus was in position at the right place and at the right time to perform every miracle the Father assigned Him. It takes genuine faith and obedience in God to perform a miracle. Jesus attended His first wedding feast in Cana which was a time of celebration and the wine was exhausted, none was left over, and the celebration was still at hand. This would be a miracle like they had never seen before. It would really be something if today's Christians would open their eyes and see miracles occurring daily all around them, especially in your own life.

The definition of a miracle is an unexpected and inviting event that is not explainable by natural or scientific laws. It is therefore considered to be the act of divine agency. Jesus' miracles were continuous after this miracle. Both Jesus and Mary realized that this miracle needed to happen at this wedding celebration to reveal who Jesus is. Jesus changed the water to wine to show his divine power and to change lives. Please understand that no one had ever changed water to wine. So, you can imagine the amazement in their minds. There was no one like Him in all the earth! Even His mother knew that He was destined for great and holy things! The miracle to change the water to wine was not for people to get drunk. It was for people to realize that a miracle maker was in their presence, and this miracle maker can and will change lives. Mary wanted everyone to see what Jesus could do. So, she asked Him to do a miracle because the wine ran out. Jesus used His power to work a miracle to witness to those present as well as the world today. His mother knew He had to do something powerful and divine. Could it be that she remembers that Jesus said that I must be about my Father's business? Mary also knew that Jesus was sent from God in heaven to her and the people. Have you ever heard of anyone else changing water to wine? I am sure you have not because only Jesus had the power to do it! His powers still exist. The evidence is everything around you.

The story will not go away because of those who witnessed it and those who tasted the wine and realized it was the best wine they ever had. It was so powerful that Jesus listened to His mother. The Son of the living God obeyed His mother and provided wine to the wedding celebration. She even knew that this would reveal who He is to those who were related and those following Him. Not only turning the water into wine stunned all the communities, it was in verse 10 as well that shocked everyone. Verse 9-10 tells us, "and the master of the banquet tasted the water that had been turned into wine. He did not realize where it had come from, though the servants who had drawn the water knew. Then he called the bridegroom aside vs10 and said, "Everyone brings out the choice wine first and then the cheaper wine after the guests have had too much to drink; but you have saved the best till now." It proves that when Jesus does something it's the best! His miracles reflect God doing His best in the life of people. It was not the wine that was central. It was Jesus changing it to prove He is the one with miracle making power. No one has ever seen anything like it. Jesus was showing His mother and those that were following Him and people at the feast His power. What does this have to do with love? Jesus is love, and He is obeying God and His mother out of love. The only ways miracles happen is through the power of God's love. Miracles are a divine demonstration of God's power.

Also remember Joseph in Matthew 1:18, who was betrothed to Mary, meaning they had a marriage by parents. This betrothal mentioned was viewed as a covenant marriage. This usually entailed waiting for consummation. In Mary's case, they had to wait almost a year to consummate their marriage. The consummation seals the marriage. Everyone that has gotten married automatically consummate their marriage regardless if it's the first or second marriage. It's called the honeymoon which is uninterrupted intimacy and love between husband and wife. Every marriage must realize that vows are real before God because it's a covenant. When angels come into your marriage it means abundant blessing are happening. An angel appeared to both Mary and Joseph to announce the coming and birth of Jesus, the Son of God. An angel told Mary that she would give birth? An angel appeared to Joseph as well and told him take Mary as his wife. Can you see it now? Jesus was the miracle baby!

It also means that God is setting you up for a miracle. Marriage means that much to God. God does miracles in birth. Jesus was birthed to do miracles. Read the story in full and see what the outcome was (Luke 2). Jesus used regular water and changed it to wine. He is our miracle maker. Every day a miracle is happening in every person's life. When Jesus gets involved, look for a miracle to happen. If you do not have a fiancée or a companion, when you get involved and in full obedience with Jesus, life as you know it will change. Jesus will cause a miracle relationship to happen in your life. You will mess around and have a Boaz and Ruth love encounter. You may have a Queen Esther experience, one night with the king. The king becomes your soul mate! You need to have an encounter with the King of Kings, Lord of Lords! His precious name is Jesus. He is far greater than any soul mate. When miracles happen, expect that it was Jesus. When miracles happen, understand that change will occur! When miracles happen, life is impacted like never. When miracles happen, God showed up and showed out! When miracles happen around you, you will bow down and worship the Lord, our God. You will recognize His miracle working power. When miracles are happening around us, souls are being saved in Jesus. Jesus is the miracle maker. Make no mistake about it; He never stops revealing miracles in our lives. I love to think on the miracles because every time a child is born, a miracle occurs. Also, every time someone is born again, it's a miracle. When children drift off and become lost, He is the miracle maker to bring that one lost child back home (Luke 15:1-7). It takes God, the true Shepherd to find and bring that one lost sheep back home.

LOVE & SATISFACTION

ISN'T SHE LOVELY, ISN'T SHE BEAUTIFUL?

SONG OF SOLOMON 4:1-7 Song of Solomon 4:1-7 How beautiful you are, my darling! Oh, how beautiful! Your eyes behind your veil are doves. Your hair is like a flock of goats descending from the hills of Gilead. Your teeth are like a flock of sheep just shorn, coming up from the washing. Each has its twin; not one of them is alone. Your lips are like a scarlet ribbon; your mouth is lovely. Your temples behind your veil are like the halves of a pomegranate. Your neck is like the tower of David, built with courses of stone; on it hang a thousand shields, all of them shields of warriors. Your breasts are like two fawns, like twin fawns of a gazelle that browse among the lilies. Until the day breaks and the shadows flee, I will go to the mountain of myrrh and to the hill of incense. You are altogether beautiful, my darling; there is no flaw in you.

I remember growing up listening to the musical artists who sing love ballads and dancing music. I was a teenager and just really enjoyed the sound and beat of the music and thinking about girls.

You see my parents had music in the house. In addition, we listened to music by Michael Jackson, Earth Wind and Fire, and absolutely Luther Vandross (love melodies) along with other old school artists. Eventually those love songs got a hold of me and I started thinking about having a girlfriend. Wow! I kept those thoughts and finally grew up and got married! I found me a wife! That was the point behind love ballads to find that special one with whom you can share your love. Jesus wants us to have one wife and one God. In the passages above, it sounds like Solomon is telling her that she is perfect in her beauty in his eyes. It seems that her beauty has such an impact on his love and attraction to her. In fact, he is telling her everything is perfect about her. He sounds like he wants to serenade her with a love ballad. It also sounds like Solomon is saying, "Isn't she lovely, isn't she beautiful? However, in this story, he wants her to know how beautiful she is. Romance is always the ticket to love. You can't beat it. Every wife needs to be romanced often. Make her feel loved! Find the most peaceful place you can take her such as Hawaii, Bahamas or some beautiful getaway vacation. Get away now from everybody for the sake of love.

Solomon's compliment is to let her know how much he thinks of her and what her beauty does to his heart. Solomon is telling her that she has all that he needs, and she lacks nothing as a woman. He tells her that he longs to be with her and her beauty ignites a fire in him to love her. Solomon seems to describe her beauty in somewhat of an odd way, but it may be a turn on in that time of love. In some respect, it has elements that will make a woman smile and love. Maybe you want to tell her, isn't she lovely, isn't wonderful. Then sing again and say isn't she lovely, isn't she beautiful. Brother King Solomon knows how to tell a woman what she has that thrills his heart and eyes. Maybe somebody's wife will understand what her husband is really saying to her. It sounds like when he gets her into a private setting, he will make it plain to her what he really means. God does not want you to make her an idol or goddess. Instead He wants you to love her and be completely satisfied. God expects her to be as submissive as she can and to satisfy her husband. But at the end of the day, the only love that can fully satisfy you is the love of God! If you live long enough, you will see what it means with the Lord and with a woman.

SOLOMON'S LOVE

1 King 11:1-13 Now King Solomon loved many foreign women. Besides Pharaoh's daughter, he married women from Moab, Ammon, Edom, Sidon, and from among the Hittites. The Lord had clearly instructed the people of Israel, "You must not marry them, because they will turn your hearts to their gods." Yet Solomon insisted on loving them anyway. He had 700 wives of royal birth and 300 concubines. And in fact, they did turn his heart away from the Lord. In Solomon's old age, they turned his heart to worship other gods instead of being completely faithful to the Lord his God, as his father, David, had been. Solomon worshiped Ashtoreth, the goddess of the Sidonians, and Molech, the detestable god of the Ammonites. In this way, Solomon did what was evil in the Lord's sight; he refused to follow the Lord completely, as his father, David, had done. On the Mount of Olives, east of Jerusalem, he even built a pagan shrine for Chemosh, the detestable god of Moab, and another for Molech, the detestable god of the Ammonites. Solomon built such shrines for all his foreign wives to use for burning incense and sacrificing to their gods. The Lord was very angry with Solomon, for his heart had turned away from the Lord, the God of Israel, who had

appeared to him twice. He had warned Solomon specifically about worshiping other gods, but Solomon did not listen to the Lord's command. So now the Lord said to him, "Since you have not kept my covenant and have disobeyed my decrees, I will surely tear the kingdom away from you and give it to one of your servants. But for the sake of your father, David, I will not do this while you are still alive. I will take the kingdom away from your son. And even so, I will not take away the entire kingdom; I will let him be king of one tribe, for the sake of my servant David and for the sake of Jerusalem, my chosen city."

One of King Solomon's issues was idolatry, the worship of false gods and shrines. Along with that a bigger issue was his love and lust for foreign women. However, his overwhelming issue was doing evil in the Lord's sight. Solomon became disobedient to God.

Culturally, you could have many wives in Solomon's time. His Father David had several wives, as well. However, God warned Solomon not to worship other gods. Solomon did not keep God's covenant, instead he disobeyed God's decrees and covenant. He got involved in marrying many foreign woman and they caused him to commit idolatry. These women that he was involved with turned his heart away from God. Do we see this in society today where a woman can turn your heart from God?

SOUL MATE

God is showing every man that a woman is supposed to help you keep your heart on God. She was created to be a helpmeet and love her husband, not be a hindrance to your life and God's purpose. Her primary ministry and job in life is to help her husband stand in the faith. She is to always serve and worship the one and true God. She is to reverence her husband. She is to be the soul mate you need for love. Because of Solomon's heart and actions to disobey God, it led to divided kingdoms. This is the beginning of the division of ten tribes of Israel (1 King 11:13, 31). Solomon broke covenant with God. His downfall was disobedience to God and lust towards women with whom he was forbidden to engage. God ripped the kingdom from him because of his disobedience and lack of honor.

Please understand that we are speaking of a man who was called the wisest man that ever lived (of course, outside of Jesus Christ). God still remembers King David, a man after His own heart and allows Solomon's son to be king over one of the tribes for the sake of David and God's chosen city Jerusalem after Solomon dies. God wants us to see that action will be taken against anyone who loves and worships another god, which is a false god. Jesus our Lord is the only true and living God. There is no one like Him!

1 Kings 11:29-33 One day as Jeroboam was leaving Jerusalem, the prophet Ahijah from Shiloh met him along the way. Ahijah was wearing a new cloak. The two of them were alone in a field, and Ahijah took hold of the new cloak he was wearing and tore it into twelve pieces. Then he said to Jeroboam, "Take ten of these pieces, for this is what the Lord, the God of Israel, says: 'I am about to tear the kingdom from the hand of Solomon, and I will give ten of the tribes to you! But I will leave him one tribe for the sake of my servant David and for the sake of Jerusalem, which I have chosen out of all the tribes of Israel. For Solomon has abandoned me and worshiped Ashtoreth, the goddess of the Sidonians; Chemosh, the god of Moab; and Molech, the god of the

Ammonites. He has not followed my ways and done what is pleasing in my sight. He has not obeyed my decrees and regulations as David his father did. God loves us deeply. Nevertheless, He will deal with those that are disobedient in His own way. We don't even have to ask God to deal with disobedience because He already knows.

Questions and Discussion:

1. Why did Ahijah tear his new cloak into twelve pieces? Explain.

_____

_____

2. List two primary things that caused the Kingdom to be torn from Solomon?

_____

_____

3. Who were the ten tribes going to?

_____

_____

4. What was done in King David's honor?

_____

_____

CHAPTER 8

A CHAMPION OF LOVE

Ephesians 5:25-26 Husbands, love your wives, just as Christ loved the church and gave himself up for her to make her holy, cleansing her by the washing with water through the word.

Love your wife and be a champion at it! I know this should make every man smile! God gave man a gift, called woman. When I think of a champion, the biblical character, Samson and the mythical character, Hercules both comes to mind. Obviously, I think of these men because of their strength and power to fight all enemies and win. The difference is that Samson's strength is a divine strength from the one and only true God. He was set apart for God's use. Hercules is a mythical character and hero. He is not real like Samson, but the television makes him look real! He displayed extraordinary strength as well. To be a champion you need the kind of strength that people will notice in case of enemy attacks. Movies show Hercules defeating two headed beast and other enemies. Nevertheless, it's not about the mythical and fictional strength in a man. It's really about the divine strength in a man, like Samson. Most people are impressed by both men's strength. Samson used the jawbone of a donkey and killed a thousand men (Judges 15:15-17). You know the word had to spread like wildfire of Samson's victory over his enemy. Later, after a failed relationship with Delilah and being blinded by the Philistines, He asked God to give him strength to defeat his enemies one last time. He ended up pushing down pillars, causing a coliseum to collapse and crumble, killing thousands. Listen Samson came back to His God where he belonged.

Husbands go into your marriage with your mind set on God and the strength and power He gives you. Know when to call on Him for help in all situations! Go into your marriage as a man of God with passion and the attitude to protect and provide for your wife and entire family. Your wife will feel secure because of your strength, passion, love for her and a strong bonded relationship.

No one else belongs in your marriage details but God! This will keep your marriage together and strong. Both of you need to be strong in the Lord if you want to be champions of love in your marriage. Champions of love must keep evil out of their marriages, such as lies, manipulation, deceit, adultery, dishonor, disobedience, and disrespect. If these traits and behaviors exist in one of the two, the marriage will have huge consequences. Anyone of these will destroy a relationship. Jesus is core to every successful relationship. Along with that relationship comes honor and respect. Men must use their divine strength like Samson in a Godly effort to defeat enemies against his marriage.

Only a Godly man with power can rebuke and conquer the devil and move on in life. Who would come up against the mighty power of God when God is on your side? If God is for you, who can be against you (Romans 8:28-38). Unfortunately, Samson failed to acknowledge His God giving in to his so-called fantasy woman and companion, Delilah. In Samson's heart, he was a champion of love and probably lust which caused him not to see clearly. His story is a story of what not to do when it comes to forming a relationship with a woman. He needed to listen to God.

He was set apart for God. His love for Delilah was not a mutual love. Delilah lied repeatedly, and she was a deceptive woman whom Samson loved very much. In her deceit, she was really a manipulator and ran a con-game on Samson. She basically had a seductive (evil) spirit over him. If Samson had obeyed God, the Lord would have provided him with the right woman.

Every man needs the right woman. A man needs her love and affection. He needs a woman with whom he can be intimate. She should be a Godly woman. If she fits that description, she will be a covenant wife in Jesus Christ. She will be a Proverbs 31 woman! Samson and Delilah's relationship failed because they did not have a covenant relationship with God together. They were not married, and they lusted after each other! Samson was infatuated with her beauty! He also disobeyed God; as she was not trustworthy. Those are the deadliest downfalls of any relationship. They contrast with the foundation of true Godly love. The champion of love and still the undisputed heavy weight champion of all creation is God! He destroyed, annihilated, and defeated the devil because of His love for humanity.

Jesus simply wants every man to show the love of God to his wife. By demonstrating Godliness to her, the relationship will become rich. The ideal marriage will exhibit oneness and flourish for a lifetime. This should be a marriage filled with the abundance of love that surpasses all things in Jesus Christ. This couple should feel like it's a relationship in paradise. I believe every couple wants an ideal marriage that will last a lifetime. If you allow God to orchestrate your marriage, with Him as the head, you can have it. Jesus is the champion of love throughout all creation. He gave himself up for the church. In the opening passage of scripture, man is admonished to love his wife just as Jesus loved the church.

Jesus's love is the source for every man. Go to Jesus when you feel broken and the marriage is in trouble. Don't let the devil in. Let Jesus back in. He wants your marriage to be a beautiful union. So, when you see each other, both of your hearts melt together. Men are to be the champion of love in your marriage. You do it by loving your wife as Christ loved the church.

Allow Jesus to lead your life. If you break from Jesus, you break from your marriage. If you are a champion after Jesus, remain a champion of love in your spiritual walk as well as in your marriage. Understand the power of Jesus' love for the church. He never gives up. His love never fails. He will not let the church fail because He is her head. Husbands are to be the head in the marriage. He is to lead with the love of Jesus, so that the two can walk as one (Genesis 2:23-24). Let Jesus be the head of your marriage. Wives let your husband be a champion! Call him champion of love! Call him your hero of love! Build him up wives! This should not be a problem especially, if you have been building up people outside of your marriage. However, don't forget, there is no higher relationship than the one with Jesus. Love helps to make everything better in the marriage overall. Jesus wants the husband and wife to champion love in the marriage. How do you do it? Ephesian 5: 22-23 tells us "Wives, submit yourselves unto your own husbands, as unto the Lord. For the husband is the head of the wife, even as Christ is the head of the church: and he is the savior of the body." Jesus is the center of all relationships especially the marriage. Jesus must be in your heart to be a champion of love for your wife and family. Love is the relationship builder and sustainer. One key piece that will help marriages is the vulnerability you have with one another. It will more than likely help you both be much freer. Vulnerability allows each person to expose areas about themselves without judgment. The spouse remains ready to help and accept the other. Jesus demonstrates covenant love to us. Just as He has a covenant with us, we should have one with each other. The covenant is a promise and agreement. It seals the relationship and makes it unbreakable.

The covenant helps the husband to be a champion with his wife. Likewise, the wife can be a champion wife to her husband. This ensures that the relationship is powerful and the love unbreakable! The husband must build up his wife as much as possible daily. Jesus is already the champion! He is the head of love. He is the Master of building people up in marriage and in life. He is the king of love. If Jesus is not in it, this entire relationship could break apart. Wives, the husband can't help but to go out of his mind when he sees your beauty.

In Proverbs 18:22 He says, "He who finds a wife finds what is good and receives favor from the Lord." The power of choice is so important. God needs to be in it. Let Him lead you in deciding who is right for you. Take heed to warnings you receive from God to stay away from the wrong match. You know it's the wrong match when behaviors do not complement each other, when spirits are not equally yoked according to the word (2 Corinthians 6:14). Seek God about it and get confirmation. Do not allow lust to override God's answer. If God is not in it, then trouble is in it. That means the enemy will cause you to fight like animals.

At one time, I was asked to conduct a wedding for this couple and during the counseling sessions, I discovered that they were both of different religions. I did not know it until the session. During the session, he claimed to be Muslim and she claimed to be Christian. There was turmoil during the counseling session. You can probably imagine what the relationship was like outside of the session. Because of his denial of Jesus, I could not conduct the wedding. Secondly, the groom would not submit to Jesus as Lord and Savior. I was not surprised at his denial. The natural man does not believe in God and what He represents. The things of God are foolish to him because he is the only one in his mind that makes sense (1 Corinthians 2:14). He is also a pride filled person. They remained in this relationship and later it did not survive. They divorced with a lot of violence and hatred! God must be the cornerstone of your relationship. A three-fold cord is not easily broken. Every man and woman desire and need peace of mind, peace in heart and a blessed marriage in Jesus name. Jesus must be central! Fall under the umbrella of Jesus Christ as Lord and Savior. This means the Holy Spirit is your guide. He requires that you must be born again (John 3:3). Don't make the wrong choice. Will you be someone unequally yoked? Will you choose someone you lust after or have true love for? Every husband is to do what God wants, not what he wants. Obey God. Recall in the previous section what disobedience did to Adam and Eve (Genesis 3:1-7). The devil broke loose in the Garden of Eden and seduced them. The word volition also comes to mind when I think of the devil's attack and sin being injected into the first man and woman that God created, Adam and Eve. The word volition means willingly and of your choice. It means the act of making a choice or decision. You have to make a conscience decision to allow the enemy to persuade you to go against God's order of love. After, Adam and Eve caved in to the devil of their own will, from that point on, marriages and relationships and the families went downhill. This all happened because they listened and acted to the voice and persuasion of Satan. Then the next thing was Cain killed his brother Abel. Sin had started its course over one disobedient act. Again, the power of choice and the devil's influence caused this murder of Abel by Cain, brother killing his brother.

The most effective way to repair or correct all of this is to accept Jesus completely in your heart, then walk in obedience. Keep a prayer life. Study the word of God, daily. If you plan to survive all the attacks of Satan and his demons, you must follow God's instructions. Adam and Eve chose to disobey God and the consequence is that all generations suffer today. This is important because your daughters and sons watch your relationship as husband and wife and they want to model your relationship. If the husband shows his wife the highest respect, the children see how happily their mother responds to it. The same is when the wife completely honors her husband in front of the children, they see it and remember it. In fact, all positive and negative behaviors will impact your children for a lifetime. Your relationship means that much to God, so model it after Jesus.

Questions and Discussion:

1. What is a champion in terms of spiritual relationship?
_____
_____

2. What will make you a better husband?
_____
_____

3. What will make you a better wife?
_____

4. What are some things you can do to make marriage better for your spouse?

_____

_____

_____

5. What does Genesis 2 say about marriage?

_____

_____

_____

CHAPTER 9

YOUR BODY: A TEMPLE

1 Corinthians 3:16-17 Don't you know that you yourselves are God's temple and that God's Spirit dwells in your midst? If anyone destroys God's temple, God will destroy that person; for God's temple is sacred, and you together are that temple.

"The Green Mile" was a movie that really touched me and I am sure it touched others as well. It was the power of love in the body unfolding! It was showing us how precious this body is. It's a temple for God to dwell inside! It seemed to be showing the power of God's love through an oversized prisoner on death row. He was in prison and had a gift from God to heal people. He used His body to remove the stench of death cause by sin from the warden's wife's body. He showed us something about the power of love from the body God gave him. The last thing on anyone's mind on death row is certainly not to heal someone else. It would be more than likely to worry about their own life and will God spare it. This prisoner wanted to be used by God. Do you want your body and gifts to be used by God? We all need to take on the attitude of this innocent man who loved God and displayed God's love through his body. Yes, your body is a temple.

When God created us, he created us as a spirit that has power, love and a sound mind. He created us in His image and likeness (Genesis 1:27). God created us as His temple. We are spirit beings that long for our Creator, God our Father. He never gave you a failed body, mind, and spirit. He never gave you a twisted or demented mind and mentality. God never created us to have a body that had all kinds of disease and mutations and sinful ways. God created us perfectly. He gave a perfect paradise to Adam. We are descendants of Adam, the first man on planet earth. In addition, God did give us authority, power, and dominion over the earth. Yes, our bodies are temples of the Holy Ghost. All are good characteristics that come from God. He also put inside of us divine strength which is remarkable. We are divine temples of the living God. He dwells inside of us. He is in many places at one time because He can do it in His power. He is God!

SOUL, BODY AND SPIRIT IN JESUS CHRIST

We are made in God's image. God perfected His creation. **"God said, Let us make man in Our image" (Genesis 1:26)**. He mentions His image and likeness. It is obvious that he would not make His image of less value. So, stop making yourself less valuable in your eyes and in the eyes of others. God made us soul, body and spirit. Jesus walked the earth soul, body and spirit. **1 Thessalonians 5:23 reads as "Now may the God of peace himself make you completely holy and may your spirit and soul and body be kept entirely blameless at the coming of our Lord Jesus Christ**. The body is just that important to God for us to take care of. Listen to this writer in **Hebrews 4:12 "For the word of God is living and active and sharper than any double-edged sword, piercing even to the point of dividing soul from spirit, and joints from marrow; it is able to judge the desires and thoughts of the heart.** This is important that every man understand that God wants man to know Him, learn of Him and follow Him. God is so passionate about it to the point that His word penetrates every area inside and out. The non-believer has issues because he does not believe the word nor believe in Jesus as the Son of God and sacrifice for sin of the world. The Apostle Paul also clearly tells us the issue of non-believers. **The natural man receiveth not the things of the Spirit of God; for they are foolishness unto him; neither can he know them, because they are spiritually discerned (1 Corinthians 2:14).** The non-believer or natural man is lost because he does not believe nor receives God's word. He is full of self-pride, self-wisdom and disobedience which heads to a down fall. Get Jesus in your life today and walk in blessings. Whatever you do as a man or woman of God, get to the receiving end of Jesus Christ. One reason that I decided to write this is because for several years I have noticed an epidemic in the form of attacks against women by Satan and his demons. This may not apply to all women; however, it does apply to an extremely large population in our society and around the world. I want you to note first what God stated about women. We know throughout the word of God, He loves women. Mary is Jesus mother and He loves his mother (Luke1, 2). Look at what God did! He created a woman to birth His only Son, Jesus Christ to save the world from destruction through His love. Mary gave birth to Jesus Christ. Jesus Christ is the Word of God. I open this chapter talking about the soul, body and spirit in Jesus Christ so that every woman, old or young, can understand the importance of surrendering themselves totally to God! Jesus talks to a woman at the well (John 4) and blessed her. He reminded her that He already knew about the five husbands and the one she currently lives with. He told her about herself because He wanted her to believe in who He was and receive His love. Notice, Jesus never placed guilt or shame on her, nor anyone he set out to heal.

Jesus tells us to remember the widow who gave her last two

coins, everything she had (Mark 12:40-44). Jesus also reminds us, in the book of Timothy, about Lois and Eunice, Timothy's mother and grandmother who were really on fire for God and raised Timothy up to know and serve God (1Timothy 1:3-7; Proverbs 22). There is also a woman who wiped Jesus feet with her hair to show reverence and humility to Him (John 13). The list goes on with perhaps thousands of women around the world that believe in Jesus as Lord and Savior. Lydia was the Apostle Paul's convert (Acts 16:14-15). Mary the mother of John Mark was a missionary with the Apostle Paul. Peter came to her home apparently for ministry (Acts 12:12). God also set up Mary Magdalene who once had seven demons within her who was set free by Jesus. Not only was she set free, she was the first person to discover Jesus' resurrection at the tomb (John 20:1-10). This is to show people in my opinion that Jesus did not misjudge, nor look down on women. He blessed women continually! There was mother Teresa who gave as much as she could to the poor in the world and left a life changing impact in the minds of millions. Her witness is phenomenal. She dedicated her life to helping others. My point is that women are assigned to multiple areas of ministry. We need to respect where God has placed a woman in ministry. She is not inferior to anyone. We should always refer to Genesis 2, 3, 4.

1 Corinthians 3:16-17 encourage us to know who dwells inside of us and that no one is to misuse their body. The Holy Spirit dwells inside of believers every moment of the day. Nothing should substitute the Holy Spirit. Demons do not have a place inside of a believer.

Avoid all these things associated with Satan's attacks on women and families. I say all of this in love that you may break every cycle and completely break loose in Jesus name! Please do not allow the enemy to lower you into being degraded into lust and self-exposure. Avoid sexual films and vulgar language. This is a major concern to families. When parents allow this kind of entertainment in the home to please their children's desires, it is harmful. Remember, you as the parents, especially mothers can break that cycle of the enemy trying to plant evil seed in your children. The father's role is to teach his family and have his wife enforce the rules.

Remember God wants to bless our entire families. It would be a blessing if Jesus was portrayed in more movies. We need to encourage people to walk in God's grace! Live the life of blessings! You were made to be blessed and not cursed! You were made to be used by God and not for evil. God wants to use you for His purpose! The Bible is clear that our bodies are the temple of God. (1 Corinthians 3:16). Women were not made to expose their bodies outside of marriage. The enemy is trying to destroy the fabric of the home. Whatever you do, your children see and believe your actions are acceptable. You are the role model in their lives. Break free today! Break free of all bondages. Do not allow anyone to convince you to do evil. What you do impacts your children for the rest of their lives! Think about it! Do what is positive in the eyes of God and your children. There are good movies with great actors male and female such as the movie, "War Room" It is a spiritual oriented movie about helping a family in need of building a better relationship" through prayer. It's about calling on God to restore a marriage. We know by now, if sex is shown on the screen, millions of people show up. When you mention Jesus, people shy away, thinking condemnation or someone is judging them. It's should be the opposite, Jesus is stretching His hands to love and restore you! He is not judging you. We pray that people show up when they hear the name of

Jesus. Jesus wants to give more love than anyone else. He is not thinking about judging you. With Jesus you get a clean slate! It's a new start and a new life! You get to become part of the family of God. We want God to be the big attraction to millions and millions of people to win souls to the Kingdom of God.

I want to encourage women to know that God calls them blessed in Proverbs 31. Her body is for God's use. Her body is for God and her husband, not the public!

God also mentions women as the "weaker vessel." She is physically not stronger than man due to her physiological makeup or design by God, in most cases. There are several strong women who lift men up, as well as the family. Nevertheless, the man is stronger. They are supposed to be one in marriage according to the word of God. He is her covering. She needs to be subject to him always. The Bible is clear in **Genesis 3:16 "To the woman he said, I will make your pains in childbearing very severe; with painful labor you will give birth to children. Your desire will be for your husband, and he will rule over you (Genesis 3:15-17)."** God is not telling husbands to dominate your wife like a floor mat. He simply wants the man to protect, cover, and guard her from all enemy attacks. She is blessed by God and her husband. The man is to take care of his wife's needs. God's plan is for both to be blessed, be fruitful and multiply (have children that will bless you). The husband is to protect and cover her because of what happened in the garden. It is more about her being aligned and in agreement with God and her husband. It's also about him being aligned with his wife, as well. She needs to know that he trusts her and vice versa. Every woman needs to understand her role. She is a wife before everything, including her profession. Her role as wife comes before any ministry. Her husband is her priority because her primary ministry is helpmeet. If her job hinders the marriage, she must make the marriage priority and adjust her career, because her husband comes first. Likewise, every man must also understand that his wife comes first. The man must be totally surrendered and under God's authority. He must take his priestly role as the head of the house.

Women are also filled with the Holy Spirit to express themselves as witnesses of the Most High God and His Kingdom. Women are anointed of God and not lesser persons. She receives the blessings from God. She is a child of the most High God. However, let's be clear, His kingdom reigns regardless of any of our service or lack of it. No one can limit how God will use His anointed women. They have maximum power from God to be used for His purpose. Women have their own spirit and must trust God the same as anyone else would! In fact, women can pray, serve, sing praises, worship and minister to God's people; and remain just as committed as men. Several women are called prophetess in the Bible and that is a powerful revelation proving that God has a purpose for women to minister in His Kingdom. God placed His anointing upon women and no man can change it! We need to break from the old traditional mindset of being boxed in and placing limits on God and His people. God said that "He will pour out His Spirit on all flesh. Your sons and daughters will prophesy" (Joel 2:28-29; Galatians 3:28-29). When it comes to the wife being a weaker vessel, it signifies and reminds the husband to be aware that he needs to cover her because Satan targets wives just like he targeted Eve. The husband needs to always cover his wife. She needs to be under his covering. If you are not in touch and in tuned with God, the enemy will use her to get the best of her husband. The enemy will try in any way he can. The enemy will try to destroy your intimate relationship. The enemy seeks to make you disobedient in your marriage and to Jesus. Jesus is just the opposite. He encourages wives to always support the husband. Husbands must do the same. Jesus encourages couples to operate as one in marriage and in prayer and keep their relationship with Jesus. He wants us to keep our spiritual hearts open to worship Him in Spirit and truth (John 4). We can rebuke the enemy in Jesus name.

I want to encourage every woman that she must have two spiritual coverings. The first covering is Jesus, and as stated before, her second covering is her husband. This gives her protection over all in her life. The relationship with Jesus primarily gives her the love that she has always longed for and is in need of daily.

Every void place can be filled in Jesus. Her second covering, her husband, the priest of the house. You are to never be above him. He is specifically appointed to be her leader. He should protect and provide for her at all costs. He is her provider through Jesus Christ. He must walk in faith, obedience and humility in Jesus Christ. He realizes that she is the weaker vessel. However, he treats her with the highest respect and honor and as an equal in the marriage. All men should recognize the unique qualities that God placed in women, especially his own wife. Learn that there are differences, but God works everything for the good of those whom He calls that love Him (Romans 8:28). Because he is a Godly man, he has insight into the workings of the enemy. God is encouraging every woman to stand her ground by using the power of prayer. Get that Lois and Eunice spirit. Get that bold spirit of Esther. Don't allow the lust of the flesh to be a center of your life. Allow Jesus to be the center of your life so the world can see you in action by the Holy Ghost. Jesus strengthens the weaker vessel and makes her stronger for His glory! Praise His name!

DEVOTION AND HONOR

THE HOLY SPIRIT BLESSING HOLLYWOOD STARS

I love devotion time in church. It is the heart of praise and worshiping God in spirit and truth. You can have devotion in your house and almost anywhere else. Devotion is an attitude of spiritual worship with enthusiasm and thanksgiving toward God. It's good to have the mindset of having fellowship with God. Open to God in songs and prayer and the word of God. Make it personal from the heart.

When I first started in the ministry, I was a deacon standing before the church with other deacons and ministers. I was in training learning how to lead devotion. After that, we humbly handed it over to the Pastor for pulpit devotion. I learned a lot during my first steps in ministry as a deacon. The lyric we sung stirred up the church congregation with the Holy Spirit leading us. We sang songs like "Victory is mine," "Hosanna Blessed Be the Rock of My Salvation," and "What a mighty God We Serve"

This next story reminded me of how awesome God is when the Holy Ghost shows up expectedly or unexpectedly. This story with Ms. Winfrey's all-star ball really shows that spiritual devotion can be anywhere God desires it to be. The essential point is the Holy Spirit and His anointing power can show up, touch and move in the life of any person or group of people. This morning I just listened to the song by Walter Hawkins entitled "Whatever it is" and a second song entitled "Marvelous" then I stumbled across a video on Oprah Winfrey's legend's ball featuring Edwin and

Walter Hawkins in which she put something together about lifting voices in praise and worshiping God. She asked from the singing artist BeBe Winans to open the program with gospel music. He starts off singing "Change" originally song by Tramaine Hawkins. Another gospel singer sang, and the next thing you know he passed the microphone around. Those who participated were recording artists Shirley Caesar, Dionne Warwick, Patti Labelle, Valerie Simpson, Chaka Khan, Yolanda Adams and Gladys Knight. They were beyond amazing! The bottom line is the Holy Spirit showed up and showed out! Its goes to show when God wants to show His presence and power, He will. He is the God of love and blessings! These legendary stars were in the spirit of the Lord on that day! They had already affected lives in their acting gifts, but now this moment was a time to give God praise using their personal talent! Most of them stated that they had never experienced anything like this. It blew me away when I thought about the power of God's love pouring out and ministering through every Hollywood star and artist in attendance. This was indeed a blessed time because the Holy Spirit showed up and delivered His goodness. You can tell by the expressions and silence of some of those in meditation, that the name of Jesus Christ was clearly on their minds and hearts. You can tell that Jesus had awakened Hollywood stars family and friends alike. Clearly people accepted that moment of devotion and joined in to praise and worship Jesus, our Lord.

Be ready! Jesus will meet you at a moment's notice! Jesus will meet you where you are! Praise His Name! You can tell by the atmosphere and expressions on their faces and body language of each person that the Holy Spirit was present. It a sign that God will be there when you praise Him! It does not matter who you are, when praises go up, blessings come down. Our Lord is the

God of love and He loves it when people praise Him. May God continue blessing and using each person in that audience and their family and friends. Glorify the name Jesus Christ as Lord! King David said it best, in Psalms 150:6, "Let everything that had breathe praise the Lord, Praise ye the Lord."

Questions:

1. Do you consider your body a temple of the Holy Spirit? Why?_____

2. What does 1 Corinthians 3:16-17 say about your body?
_____

3. What bible characters realize they were filled in the spirit?_____
_____
_____

4. What does 1 Corinthians 2:14 tell us?_____
_____
_____

CHAPTER 10

A TRUE CHRISTIAN SOLDIER

It was late one night when my wife suggested to we watch one of the movies I picked up the night before. My mind was somewhere else wondering what God wanted me to minister the next day for Sunday church service. I went to my home office and started looking at some scriptures and had for the most part believed God had already given me what I needed to preach for Sunday. That is not always the case. The Lord God always has something powerful and unique on His agenda. We must learn to put our agenda to the side and let God have his way. Nothing is ever anointed or ordained until God says so. I thought the movie was half way finished. I went into the living room and the movie had basically just started. The movie was about a combat medic who did not want to touch a weapon, but he did want to serve in the military to save lives. He beat the court marshal and everyone against him and was granted permission by a brigadier General, who recited the constitution for a conscientious objector. Also, you may not ever judge a book by its cover again once you read and understand this story of a real Soldier.

You never know who a person really is until God reveals them in a way you may have not expected. PVT Doss had bad experiences with the soldiers and the command in the unit he was assigned to. He was ridiculed and picked on. It was not until he performed on the battle field in the position as a combat medic, a position in which he was deeply passionate. PVT Desmond Thomas Doss remained on Hacksaw Ridge with his company during the worst of the battle. Even after losing over a hundred men in the war against the Japanese, he remained the only single soldier on top of Hacksaw Ridge. He believed he was directed by God to rescue and save lives. He was on the ridge saving all the wounded soldiers throughout the night and the next day. Even when cover was broken, and he was under direct gun fire, he continued to pull the wounded to safety, by lowering them to the point below the ridge using a rope. His unit commander did not know until the next day that he was still alive on the ridge lowering wounded men to safety. Even in his brokenness he held to his values and principles not to use a weapon to kill. He still set out to rescue his fellow soldiers while unarmed on a ridge under heavy artillery fire of the Japanese army all around him. This kind of act of bravery is so remarkable and unheard of by one single man. PVT Doss is beyond incredible. He was a God sent miracle amid combat where men were killing each other, and the devil was in the midst of the killing. His actions were glorious in the sight of God. I could not help but to think that He had an angel with him because this is unheard of. He was awarded the Medal of Honor for his actions in World War II in which he saved the lives of 75 men single-handedly with no weapon. I thought I had seen a lot in this world until this movie made it into my living room called Hacksaw Ridge. (Warning: this movie has a lot of combat and severe graphic images of violence). Although, I never met him before, this soldier has made it into my heart because of what he has done as a true Christian soldier. This man believed and loved the Lord with all his heart! It's impossible to miss his witness of the Lord through his actions. He listened to God and acted on it! You don't see this kind of heroics anywhere. This kind of bravery and love for God and country is beyond words! We know that he was a Godly hero. His heroic actions are indeed miraculous. While on the ridge, he prayed to God to show him what to do after everyone else had left and climbed down the ropes. He received his answer and saved as many men as he could. You knew it was a miracle from God because he spoke to God constantly, asking God to just give him strength and show him how to save another one. He would repeat the same statement to God; "Let me save another one Lord!"

PVT Doss is indeed the model and epitome of a Christian soldier of the Lord serving with a true heart! I am inspired by his devotion and honor to God. He has left an impact that is etched into my heart and spirit as a fellow soldier for our Lord, Jesus Christ. One reason he impacts my heart is because his defining moment in life was allowing Jesus to use him in combat to save lives. All of those soldiers in his company trusted him and believed in him and his God, even his Company Commander believed in him as a preacher I need that kind of endurance, devotion and attitude to speak and believe in the Lord, "Let me save one more." I want to keep saying it over again as I drag lost soul one after the other to Jesus for salvation (eternal life), healing and deliverance. I can imagine and believe that God has spoken to Corporal Doss saying, "Well done good and faithful servant." Sometimes we can underestimate people and what God has done and how God will use them. God knows how to lift people up when they are down and when it looks like they are defeated. Praise and worship the name of Jesus Christ, the Son of the Living God forever and ever. Our Lord never lets us down. He is constantly rescuing people every day and moment of life. Lord, we give you praise! Jesus is Lord!

DEVOTION AND HONOR

Romans 12:10 Be devoted to one another in love. Honor one another above yourselves.

Devotion is a powerful word when it comes to relationships, service and in occupations. How often do you find a couple truly devoted to one another? How often do you find a true professional devoted to his/her craft? The definition of devotion is displaying love and loyalty and, in a sense, enthusiastically performing things for a specific purpose. Another way of looking at devotion is giving your all into something that really matters to you in heart. Serving and worshipping Jesus is a priority. The key thing in life is to be devoted to worship our Lord, God in Jesus name!

The movie, "Hidden Figures" just made a special person in my life so happy and excited! She gave the movie high accolades, 5 stars! I finally got the chance to watch it with her. The movie reflects a time of division, racism and segregation. African American women were shown as overcomers, reaching one of the highest accomplishments in NASA. The thing that impressed me was that these ladies accomplished their missions with the highest of honors. They used their skills and superiority of knowledge to work to advance the astronauts and the NASA space program. Katherine Johnson, Dorothy Vaughan and Mary Jackson are the three brilliant African-American women who served as the brains at the forefront of NASA's major space operations. In one of the scenes, I was totally blown by Katherine Johnson (played by actor Taraji P. Henson. She was a scientist and mathematical genius. She memorized and wrote on boards highly important space scientific mathematic equations revealing accurate calculations supporting orbit and return "GO" results.

Everyone in the conference room was shocked. At one point one of the most famous astronauts directly requested her to calculate the key numbers using her mind (intelligence) because the computer had it wrong, but she had it correct. Her calculations were correct, on the money and perfectly worked! This astronaut had complete confidence in her before he went out of space. When you think about it, she was not just making history as an African American Woman; she was showing the world in some respect her ability. It was their devotion that caused them to stand out. They had the desire to be the best at what they knew! Octavia Spenser and Janelle Monae were remarkable in their roles in revealing an attitude of never give up on what you believe in. God made all three of these women to operate at the highest degree of excellence.

When it comes to Christianity, following Jesus Christ as Lord we find that the Apostle Paul can easily be the epitome of devotion to Jesus Christ. He devoted his entire life to serving, evangelizing and preaching Jesus Christ immediately upon his conversion. Surely, there are other Christians in the Bible and around the world with a similar commitment to serving and worshiping Jesus Christ. Commitment is rare within Christianity because of the challenges and fear that are presented. The Apostle Paul wrote two-thirds of the gospel and much of it was written in prison while under persecution. His letters alone exemplify his devotion to our Lord, Jesus Christ. Almost every scholar would without hesitation agree that the Apostle Paul's is one of the greatest men of God ever known! Holy men from various religious affiliations have read and studied God's word through the Apostle Paul's writings.

The word devotion is a critical word in relationships because it denotes a since of loyalty. It also spells out an unwavering level of commitment and obedience to the one you love or married. Many people make devotion and honor to one another so difficult, when most of the time it's easy. It is always heart breaking when a wife does not exhibit devotion and honor from her heart to her husband. She must be inclined to his needs when it comes to intimacy, social connection, friendship, etc. It is not a one-way street, likewise her husband must cater to her needs in every way. (1 Corinthians 7). Truth be told, the only thing that will matter the most in this lifetime is your relationship with Jesus, your wife and husband, and the remainder of your family. Jesus changes everything when you become devoted to Him.

Honor is powerful because it teaches us to respect and encourage others. Honor reminds us to lift someone else above yourself. The word honor means high respect, to regard with great respect and esteem according to the dictionary. Honor is not putting anyone on a pedestal but giving proper recognition to a person deserving of it. A wife should recognize her husband each day by honoring Him. This mean she gives him the highest respect period! She should really focus on treating him like a king. Do not skip a day honoring your spouse (Ephesians 5). You honor him by the things you do for him and the time you spend talking with him intimately. A wife should cheer for her husband when he is doing something, whether it's repairing something around the house, exercising, playing basketball, or serving in ministry. A wife is her husband's cheerleader! Don't ever forget it! When you neglect this important duty and he sees you cheering for someone else, he will feel betrayed and believe that you are not loyal to him. Without honor in the house, the relationship is broken, and the house is unstable and out of order. With honor, the presence of paradise is in the house! The enemy seeks to come in and stir up misunderstanding in your family and marriage. If you stick to following Ephesians 5, which has directions for husbands and wives, your marriage will be strong and honorable. There is power in honor. If you see what Revelations 4 shows us regarding honoring God, it will change your perception and perspective of what honor looks like. One simple scene of God will change your world. The 24 elders are around God's throne giving honor, glory, and thanksgiving. As they worship Him, they cast their crowns to the Lord (Revelation 4**)**. All honor and glory go to God from you and me, every day. In fact, make it a habit when you wake up in the morning, fall on your knees and lift our Father in Heaven in Jesus's name daily. Remember, you never ever glorify or give honor like this to anyone else besides God, otherwise you find yourself in idolatry.

Questions and Discussion:

1. Share your definition of 'devotion'.

_____

_____

2. Who are you devoted to?

_____

_____

3. When will you be devoted to Jesus Christ and His Father in Heaven?

_____

4. Are you willing to devote your life to Jesus?
_____

5. What is the importance of devotion to you?
_____
_____
_____

6. How do you view devotion in family?

_____

_____

CHAPTER 11

DEVOTION AND HONOR

DR. MARTIN L. KING, JR.

I found myself writing a note after the worst remarks made were echoed throughout the world by a world leader in America's highest office. I found it necessary to address it in this book. My initial thought was to send it to NBC, CBS, ABC, CNN, HLN, USA, MTV, TNT, TBS and other news broadcasts around the world. I wanted congressional leaders to put a stop to this negative world leader. They should keep him from destroying the country and the world with his rhetoric spewed out before crowds and through social media. We want nuclear weapons destroyed and disposed of right now as a measure to save the world from self-destruction. I also want every nation to know that millions of Americans do not agree with the negative, racially derogatory and degrading comments this world leader has sent out. Our hearts seek peace and love around the world.

Please understand that we are under God's power, mercy, His love and forgiveness. This world is supposed to be a better place for all people. Love is the most powerful source that exists in humanity. In fact, Humanity exist because of love. Every person on the earth wants to be loved. We need love to stabilize the world especially during times when man misuses his power. Every year we celebrate Dr. Martin L. King Jr. as a holiday, remembering the struggle of racism, inequality and injustice and how far we have come in this country and abroad. Perhaps his most famous speech "I have a Dream" still echoes throughout the world, certainly in America. More than anything else in Jesus Christ, Dr. King was advocating that all people live together God's way in freedom and love regardless of any racial and cultural differences. Now more than ever before, we need to apply what Dr. King has contributed to all people around the world. Dr. King was driven by God to echo freedom through Jesus Christ to all men! Freedom, peace and love needs to be at the forefront of every world leader's mind and do not let anything contaminate it. Dr. King spoke powerfully in so many speeches. One of his speeches echo in my heart when he said, "Let Freedom Ring" The world needs continued stabilization in peace and freedom. Only peaceful words bring freedom. Men and women in Jesus Christ help to spread that peace and freedom we all need! The world does not need nuclear adversaries. Every nation need to dispose of its nuclear weapons. Compliance is of urgency around the world! Look into the eyes of your children in your country! Look at your position in your country! Let freedom ring! In fact, the arms race between countries should be eliminated. One should admire the efforts of Dr. King to help restore and save Humanity from its own self-destruction and demise. The one sure way of doing this as he spoke of, defeating nuclear arms and war around the world which is the enemy and threat of world peace and life.

We pray that every country around the world the United States, Russia, Korea, China, Africa, Haiti, Great Britain, France and every country in this world hinge on peace and freedom applying what we have learned from Dr. King's lessons and movement of non-violence, equal Justice, peace, love and freedom for Humanity. This is the time to be vigilant in peace within all governments, presidents, monarchy to lay down and destroy every nuclear weapon arsenals and force for the sake of love, peace and humanity. In fact, destroy all nuclear capabilities throughout the world and make this world a better place to live in freedom, not fear, freedom not terrorism, freedom that all men are created equal under God. It is important to remember that the Emancipation Proclamation by Abraham Lincoln was passed through order in January 1, 1863. It was written to stop slavery and set people free. This emancipation set a way of life and is always to be enforced just as the original framers of the Constitution of the United must be adhered to. Both the Emancipation proclamation and the Constitution primary goal is to keep order, preserve freedom, democracy, maintain the highest of ethics and provisions to humanity and life itself.

The United States of America is the head of the world powers. The United States of America does not desire nor expect an invasion on America's soil. World peace is always the priority of this the United States of America. The expectation is that other country comply with the Treaty of Versailles signed 28 June 1919. This peace treaty was sign at the end of World War I by allied nations and Germany at Hall of mirror inside the palace of Versailles, France. Germany was subjected to several penalties and restriction in which some believe impacted the rise of Adolf Hitler. This government and citizens of the United States of America need to understand that this country is at jeopardy or at risk of Russia and/or North Korea nuclear arsenal attacks. Either one Russia or North Korea would love to invade this country and make all Americans prisoner of slave camps just like Hitler did with the Jews. If you recall watching the old Patrick Swayze movie of 1984 "Red Dawn" which gave us ideas of what America would look like to some extent if Russia had invaded America by surprise. Mr. Swayze's character and a small band of Warriors got together and fought back against this evil. The problem in America today is that the people have not risen to make this government stand tall and be accountable! If the people rise and fight against this political system that's dragging the country down and damaging our National Security in this white house (2017-2018), we are susceptible to a threat being successful. Our leaders are exposing us to the jaws of the enemy by not doing their jobs of protecting and preserving the United States. Listen, we need 100% National Security in place as well as a strong leader uncompromising and cares about all people in the United States and around the globe. We need a country that people will stand up against tyranny and hate. The Unites States does not have time to be divided as Russia and North Korea observes and plots to attack with nuclear arms of destruction. The people need to pray to Jesus Christ for repentance, covering, protection, righteousness, honor and thanksgiving to God, our father. Pray against all attack, foreign and domestic and that this country will not be held hostage by the grips of the devil and adversaries, including Russia and North Korea.

We also need to understand that the Bible tells us in 1 Peter 5 that there's an enemy who seeks after us as a roaring lion that he may devour us. We know war is inevitable, so we must be prepared always! People need to know that the enemy's plot is to divide and place evil in the hearts of every leader and person throughout the world. The enemy desires to inflict evil and stir it up with countries against one another. It's time to take a stand and every Government around the globe. God put government leadership in place for a reason. One is to lead people and be obedient and honorable to God (Roman 13). Every President and head leader with supporting cabinets and staff representative of government throughout need to come together in peace and harmony. The world needs unity and no division. The world needs people who stand for the better of humanity and peace.

Dr. King was a man of devotion and honor. I sincerely believe that God gave Dr. Martin Luther King this sermon and speech, "I Have a Dream "to shape American and the word in God's order of peace and freedom. He also gave one of the most important visionary God led sermons ever on April 3, 1968 "I've been to The Mountain Top." In this Mountain Top sermon, Dr. King hit so many facet and global point of life. He knew exactly how to emphasize God's deliverance from Egypt much like African Americans and white American needed deliverance from racism and slavery. It is poison, a plague, and contaminates the very root of man's soul and spirit. Only God can remove it! Jesus used Him to point us to the Good Samaritan actions to help one another as opposed to the priest and Levite who stepped on the other side and people that would leave you for dead. Just as important, God gave the world this great Man of God to help set captives free in every ethnic group and culture from slavery, racism, and injustice. Dr. King left a mark unforgettable in world History. The power of nonviolence overshadows the stain and engrained hate and evil. God used Him to change the mentality, character, soul and spirit of people throughout the world. Saints, one man can make a difference and change government and the world under God.

We need governments in every country to stand down and surrender to Jesus Christ for the sake of peace for in every family and household, and in every culture all around the world. We must believe that we are in God's will when we act out in obedience to what God ask of us. We must please Him. We must believe that it was God who used past leaders, Presidents in every country for peace and stability. We must ensure peace, tranquility and the balance for the sake of a better humanity through the world.

Likewise, I want to talk about Moses because He was truly a Man of God devoted and Honorable in the site of God. Moses lifted the serpent on a cross, so people could look upon it and be healed. St John 3:14 concluded with the fact that our eyes need to be stayed on the cross where Jesus was nailed to death and he took away the sin much like in numbers 21. Everything was taken away through healing and deliverance. Moses lifted the serpent so that people could look at and be healed. The point of it is that the entire world would need to look to Jesus on the cross and believe in His redemption of sin and be healed and delivered. Another point of it is that a world filled with evil and hate would look at Jesus on the cross crying out to His Father that "It is Finished." God also desire that man in his most delicate, fragile and sinful nature would look inside the tomb and visualize Jesus being raised from the dead by the glory of His Father. There comes a point in time that man will have to look to Jesus for His life and understand that He is accountable for all his action and word. God reminds us that He is always victorious, and it's finished. The Lord our God reminds us when He said "He would bruise that serpents head, Jesus did it all in the name of our Father in Heaven. God did not create us to kill off the human race. He created us with the power of love. He created us to demonstrate and spread love. His purpose for every person in His Kingdom is to spread the love of Jesus Christ.

ROOTED IN THE LOVE OF MONEY

1 TIMOTHY 6:10 For the love of money is the root of all evil: which while some coveted after, they have erred from the faith, and pierced themselves through with many sorrows.

Devote your heart to God first and foremost. Devotion is truth and honor, and a pure heart exalting God only! It will save you from other elements in the world that seek to put you in bondage and so easily entangle you like mammon (money). Money is definitely perhaps the number 1 item along with sex in society that gets to the heart and soul of millions of people. Money impacts the world because men allow it inside the heart (Matthew 6:21).

Upfront, the Bible is not describing the money as evil. It is pointing to the heart of man having love for it which causes many problems like divorce, murdering and other evil things in the world. Money is meant to be used for the good in exchange for goods between people in the market place. One of my experiences in witnessing the love of money is observing gamblers on a street shooting dice to win the mega bucks! One time it got so heated because one the neighborhood brother was hitting all the right numbers and the others did not like it. Then an argument broke out and shooting begun and the winner got shot and did not make it out. He was a cool brother, but he enjoyed shooting dice and being in that hood environment taking a risk! One big problem that night like so many others was the love of money. When you are gambling like that you can almost feel the power of money being rooted in someone else. Do not fall in love with money! What you fall in love with has your heart captured in some way or another. The heart can become so wicked and overwhelmed with the love of money. Lives and families change for the good or the bad depending on the love of money in your life. Do not allow your life to be full of greed with the love of money. The love of money is the root of evil. In Acts 5 a married couple died because they held back from giving to God. This is not a scare tactic. Read the scripture Act 5 as it says. "Acts 5:1-6 Now a man named Ananias, together with his wife Sapphira, also sold a piece of property. With his wife's full knowledge he kept back part of the money for himself, but brought the rest and put it at the apostles' feet. Then Peter said, "Ananias, how is it that Satan has so filled your heart that you have lied to the Holy Spirit and have kept for yourself some of the money you received for the land? Didn't it belong to you before it was sold? And after it was sold, wasn't the money at your disposal? What made you think of doing such a thing? You have not lied just to human beings but to God." When Ananias heard this, he fell down and died. And great fear seized all who heard what had happened. Then some young men came forward, wrapped up his body, and carried him out and buried him. This is what made me start ensuring my tithe and giving was to God and nothing withheld. I also 1 Corinthians 9:6-7. Make sure you love God and your family more than money. Money itself is a means of transfer and purchasing power for people to receive goods. It is not evil and it is not the root of evil. The love of money is the root of evil. It's original use stem from trading and giving something to receive something in the early civilization. Nevertheless, tensions were always up high as they are in today's society when dealing with money. For example, I was trying to purchase a home in New Jersey. I was relaxed throughout the process even though I did not have the other money on hand at the time. Nevertheless, I knew that the money was coming because I had faith in God that he wanted me to have it. I had absolutely no doubt about it coming in time. My lender was the opposite. He had almost developed high blood pressure and a temper and lack of patience, over eagerness just because he wanted to see the remaining funds. My point is he even developed a negative and hostile behavior which I never forgot because he worried so much about the money. All the money came and we purchased the home which was a mansion. I am sure all of those attacks on him and against me fell off immediately when the money came in. Other quick example areas that people need to address where evil attack over money. If you don't address it, you can fall victim to it. There are gangsters that kill people over money. There are drug dealers that create a violent and deadly situation if money is not paid for those drugs they are selling. There are families and marriages that divide and divorce over money. There are people that rob others to get more money. There are people that cheat and manipulate over money. Those are major areas where the love of money effect people lives. Have you heard of the rich ruler encounter with God? In Luke 12:18-20, "And he said, This will I do: I will pull down my barns, and build greater; and there will I bestow all my fruits and my goods. And I will say to my soul, Soul, thou hast much goods laid up for many years; take thine ease, eat, drink, and be merry. But God said unto him, Thou fool, this night thy soul shall be required of thee: then whose shall those things be, which thou hast provided? If you fall into one of those categories above, get out of it. Ask the Lord, Jesus to help prioritize your life. God to Jesus Christ is prayer and ask Him to move you out of that situation. God made money to be a blessing, not to fight and kill over green paper. It was made for consumer and purchasing power, meaning to get goods for your family and pay to price for the goods. Nevertheless, money is also mention in the Bible in Malachi 3:8-10 in giving tithe. There are other areas such as

Genesis 14:20, Genesis 28:20-22, Leviticus 27:30- 32, 2 Corinthians 9:6-7, Hebrew 7:5-9, Matthew 23:23, Luke 18:12, Luke 11:42 and Proverbs 3:9. I believe God open the power of giving to Him so that men will not allow greed to dominate them and at the same time give offerings and what God required to release greed from the heart. It was also to support the finances of the local church and priest and pastors that shepherd God's house of prayer. The power of God's love is the only thing that can break the power of anything else in your life. He already broke Satan and sent him to hell. What more do you want from God in your life? He can do it.

Questions & Discussion

1. What does it mean to give to God?

_____
_____

2. Which scripture helps you the most in giving?

_____
_____

3. Which word is the most powerful to you in this scripture above?Why?

_____
_____
_____

CHAPTER 12

LOVE IS PATIENT, LOVE IS KIND!

1 Corinthians 13:4-5 Love is patient, love is kind. It does not envy, it does not boast, it is not proud. It does not dishonor others, it is not self-seeking, it is not easily angered, it keeps no record of wrongs.

It's so amazing how one person can treat another person with love and it makes a lasting impact for the rest of that person's life. Show kindness and patience in love today. The power of love is embedded in scripture. When you demonstrate patience with other people it's a way to show love. It is important because usually people run out of patience, going off on the deep end with violence or some other unnecessary behavior. It can end up destroying a person whose soul could have been won into God's Kingdom. Our Christian walk in love matters much more than we know. God is always distributing love in some way or another. Walking in love is something that is remarkable. You can bless others when they really see that reflection in Christians. One of the hardest things to do is accept someone chewing you out for no reason. The right way to respond is in humility and never let the misunderstanding get under your skin. That's patience in action. I do want to make it crystal clear that Christians are not perfect and have great challenges, as well. The Christian needs the Holy Spirit to walk in love. One act of kindness, like giving food or clothing to someone in need can impact a person for life.

Delivering a meal to the elderly is another kind act. Allowing someone to go ahead of you in line because they really need to get somewhere is a kind act. Being a courteous driver in rush hour is also a kind act. You can help someone who has fallen to stand back up.

Of course, this is the Christian way to help catch those that have fallen away from God and help them get back to our Heavenly Father. Love does not hold on to past grudges and hate. The reason people hold on to that kind of poison is because they are keeping records of wrongs. God wants us to delete all recorded offense. If you have a relative that you don't want to see because of wrong doings, delete that thought from your memory bank with love. It is an act of kindness when you let offenses go. You can release a person out of the mental prison that you held them in. I don't know about you, but it certainly sounds familiar to me. I pray Lord release me from any unclean spiritual thought and grudge. Today in the name of Jesus, that strong hold is gone.

Love will force you to reveal truth in all circumstances to yourself and others. Leave no stone unturned. Your heart can't stand lying. It must surrender to the truth. God's word is truth. Admit that all troubles and heartaches are over. Healing must take place in Jesus name. We are reminded that everything will fail except love. Everything else will fade away. But love will never fail nor depart from us.

Questions:

What does 1 Corinthians 13:4 say regarding love? _____

What does 1 Corinthians 13:5 say regarding love? _____

MARRIED AND IN LOVE!

Ephesians 5:33 However, each one of you also must love his wife as he loves himself, and the wife must respect her husband.

When you obey this scripture, you will know that your marriage and relationship is in good standing. You will have peace of mind and heart! Keeping the first love attitude can keep your relationship strong. When you keep love alive with romance on a daily or weekly basis, it distributes the power of joy and peace in the relationship.

Respect is in the highest order and expectation from God. When you show respect to your spouse, he/she will tend to go beyond the ordinary to make you happy and feel blessed! Your spouse will cherish you! When you give them proper attention, it activates a new freshness in the relationship. Attention is not optional in your relationship. It sends continuous and positive sentiments. Anything opposite is destructive! This kind of love elevates your marriage with a new level of intimacy in your relationship. You need to take on the mind that it's about you and your spouse only! The, actions you take, the respect and honor you show have the greatest impact when God is in it!

When a couple love each other, like Jesus said husbands ought to love their wives, their love is unstoppable. Demons tremble at this kind of marriage because Jesus is the center of it! The devil will fear this kind of love because God is in it!

Love is powerful. Couples should get married when they are in love! Pray that no one gets married out of convenience. Convenience can lead you down a different path. Don't put out the good fire and flames in your marriage! Keep the fires burning so the relationship will remain strong and in tack! Don't even think about your marriage ever dying! Keep it alive! Keep a positive attitude toward it. Think about what you can do next to make it better. Purchase her some flowers. You can do it! With this kind of attitude, will elevate and steer your marriage to new levels of love. It only gets better. When you respect one another, it destroys bondages, and anything that hinders the marriage. Block out demons that want to destroy you. You can shield your relationship against principalities and all darkness. Respect simply strengthens the marriage each day it's offered. In the passage below a man and women is speaking the language of love. This is the kind of language that helps marriages. In Song of Songs 1:1-4 Let him kiss me with the kisses of his mouth— for your love is more delightful than wine. Pleasing is the fragrance of your perfumes; your name is like perfume poured out. No wonder the young women love you! Take me away with you—let us hurry! Let the king bring me into his chambers. It sounds like much romance going on in this passage. It sounds like the heat is turned up. The husband is a king. Let him bring the wife into the bedroom chambers and let love spark! Make him know that he is a king in her eyes. Many words don't have to be spoken, just enough! Remember, actions speak louder than words. The husband will let the wife know that she is his Queen.

I recently turned my computer on and saw a couple who was on the beach coming out of the water. Someone commented on them being opposite in appearance. When I saw the couple, I couldn't help but to think about how happy they were in that photo. There was another comment as to how beautiful the wife was and how her husband liked everything about her. Amen! That's how a brother should feel! That is exactly what marriage relationships should be. If your marriage is not demonstrating any this type of love, someone in the marriage is depriving the other. Don't withhold out loving comments. Don't hold out on anything with your spouse. It is not God's will. If you do, then you are acting in accordance with the enemy you are one in Jesus Christ (Genesis 2, 1 Corinthians 7 and Ephesians 5). Remember, it's how you respect and treat your husband and your wife. It takes three to get this right! Husband, wife and Jesus as your source of strength in this love cord.

CHAPTER 13

THE LOVE GPS
(GLOBAL POSITIONING SYSTEM)

1 Corinthians 13:1-7 If I could speak all the languages of earth and of angels, but didn't love others, I would only be a noisy gong or a clanging cymbal. If I had the gift of prophecy, and if I understood all of God's secret plans and possessed all knowledge, and if I had such faith that I could move mountains, but didn't love others, I would be nothing. If I gave everything I have to the poor and even sacrificed my body, I could boast about it; but if I didn't love others, I would have gained nothing. Love is patient and kind. Love is not jealous or boastful or proud or rude. It does not demand its own way. It is not irritable, and it keeps no record of being wronged. It does not rejoice about injustice but rejoices whenever the truth wins out. Love never gives up, never loses faith, is always hopeful, and endures through every circumstance.

How often do things affect other people's lives? People are impacted more often than one might think. Your actions make a difference! Don't take it lightly especially when dealing with love! Love works in Jacks story and exploration below. In this one story, you can apply so many of love characteristics. This will challenge your relationship as a Christian. Locate all challenges below and make a checklist to see if you can make a difference using Exodus 3. See yourself at your altar.

Helen Holms was attending church while her husband was stationed in Fort Hood, Texas. The church was called Christian Worship Outreach Center. It was a mon-denomination church. She was in the choir and her husband was the Pastor and giving his Sunday sermon entitled "Let the Fire Burn" using Exodus 3. He was talking about how Moses was appointed by Adonai (God). The Holy Spirit used him to deliver the message. After the service, a self-proclaimed prophetess told Helen that God was using her husband, Jack. Then Jack came over and joined in. Prophetess Sarah Townsend told Jack and Helen that they were not to allow evil deception and spiritual blocks to get in the way of God's plan. The woman who claimed to be a prophetess affected Jack and Helen in just that moment! Words affect people! Spirituality has effects on people to either draw them or cast a negative impression. Prophetess Sarah stated that God was about to use Jack to deliver some people out of bondage today after church. Three hours later as they were coming out of a shopping mall, a family with four children stopped Jack and asked for prayer. Jack knew Raymond Horne from an old job, but he never met the family. Jack prayed for them on the spot. Jack prayed a prayer of deliverance. He spoke in the prayer that they were to take a stand and rebuke things that are not of God (Deuteronomy 18:20; Ephesians 4:29; Proverbs 18:21). He prayed to release the deliverance power God used in Egypt to set His children free from bondages (Exodus 3). Raymond mentioned afterwards that he felt like he had been set free. He stated simply, for some reason, he does not feel like he was held captive any longer. Prayers change lives. The Herbert family was passing by and heard the prayer of deliverance and asked Jack what church he attended? Jack stated that he attends Christian Worship Outreach Center where there is high praise and worship of our Lord, Jesus Christ! More importantly, the word of God is delivered. You want to be affected by the word of God! The following Sunday, Raymond attended the church and his entire family came up at the invitation to receive Jesus in their heart. Raymond also testified that many of his urges had left and something had come over him. Raymond stated that he felt free, like a new man. The Herbert family also brought along three other families to church with them, all because they heard the prayer outside of the shopping mall. They thought it was bold that someone would be praying outside. To their amazement, all three couples received Jesus as Lord and Savior at the invitation.

Words in our prayers affect people. The words in our prayers are like a GPS that direct people back to God. Don't under estimate the power of prayer and deliverance. Everything Jack was doing was under the inspiration and love of Jesus Christ. You see chains were being broken. When God sets something in motion, blessings will happen, and curses will be broken. Speak a word and let the Spiritual GPS take hold of it and guide someone back to Jesus. We need to speak the word of God to stop the enemy from placing curses on our families. Stop him in his tracks. Then give God all the glory. His power delivers.

LOVE DEEPLY AFFECTS YOUR MARRIAGE

The core foundation of any marriage is love. Other key elements are trust, communications and honor. The love GPS helps marriages in a variety of ways. So many things work different for so many people. Some things are not just set the same as the next couple. We need direction and guidance in marriage by the Holy Spirit. Bring love to the forefront of your marriage. Use the Lord's love as a GPS. The Holy Spirit is your GPS love guide. Love finds its way through anything because of God!

Helen learned to encourage and stick by her husband's side until his last day on earth. How? It was the love GPS that directed her. Don't allow the enemy to make you fall short. The key is hearing from God and being obedient. The entire story of Moses at the burning bush revolves around obedience and responding to the call as a deliverer. This is why we need to turn on the love GPS. The love GPS helps us to strive to speak positive words. Speaking positive life-giving words bring love into the atmosphere. Because Jack's wife stood by his side, He was encouraged and begin making progress in the ministry. People lives were being changed. He became a better minister of Jesus Christ. Always stand up for what you believe is right. Don't let things get you down or run you from the ministry. Live for Jesus. As you live for the Lord, You walk in the blessed life as you encourage yourself in Jesus Christ. Joseph had to encourage himself and it lead him to be the second highest in authority over Egypt. You guessed it right! He went from the pit to the palace. Use the word of God to encourage yourself. You must focus on living for Jesus and reigning with Him forever!

Love has the power to affect us in so many ways in our lives. Every person experiences a moment in life when they know someone else affects them! It is usually due to twist and turns that impact our love for one another. Nevertheless, love is needed in our lives. Love has a way of changing things, turning things around and ultimately releasing blessings in abundance. We simply may not have survived many issues, situations or circumstances if it had not been for the love of Jesus. Love never reflects envy. Love is not too proud to admit mistakes and it does not exhibit a prideful spirit! The Apostle lists several characteristics that are never missed in our daily living. One of the most powerful characteristics of love is the fact that "Love never fails." Love is powerful and perfect because it comes from God. Love is permanently engraved in our spirits and heart! If you want to experience love, keep trusting God. You can't hide from love. God is love! (John 4) If you give God a chance to help you, He will. Trust Him and watch Him work. Everyone in creation experiences love because it's in God's plan. The Holy Spirit helps us to be patient. We don't have to rush things in life because love is patient. Often maturity relates to patience. There is no need to hurry. Put your mind at peace. Let the Holy Spirit guide you into it.

The Holy Spirit will also guide you to honor your parents. He will guide the wife to honor her husband and the husband also to love her like Jesus loves the church. When you show honor, you demonstrate the power of love. Around the throne of God, the elders give God honor and glory (Revelation 5:13)! When you love God, you glorify Him. Love does not seek its own glory! Love does not seek to impress others. Love is not involved in a popularity competition.

However, if you want to witness, you should show love. People will know you by your fruit and witness the love of Jesus Christ. Love is not counting your mistakes or anyone else's. In fact, love erases and releases those things that entangle you or block your blessings. Love forgives wrongs. God does not want us to recall old things. Love forgets it and never brings it back up!

Love always protects, trusts, hopes and perseveres. God wants us to trust Him. Don't stop because of other people. You persevere because you have hope and desire to please God. Love gives you the power to forgive and move ahead in life. Love rebukes and pushes evil out of your life. Love rejoices with truth. Love has all power in it. Love is positive thinking. Love is positive actions. Love is aligning yourself in Jesus because He is the Son of God and He cares for you. Love is reigning with Jesus Christ.

I believe that God is showing us that He passes before us on so many occasions and we do not acknowledge Him. We miss His presence. We just get in a prideful way and block out what God is showing us. Until we really understand that we need Him and can't live without Him, we will continue to miss out on God's presence. He passes before us when we are in hurting situations, when there is no one else to cry or lean on. He comes to wipe the tears away. He passes before us when it seems like the enemy may have the victory. But God comes by and delivers healing. He delivers miracles. He delivers sight to the blind, He delivers whatever you need in your life. Blind Bartimaeus, a blind beggar heard that Jesus was passing by and he called on Jesus to have mercy on him. He was sitting on the roadside where people were passing by all day and night. But when heard of Jesus, he was bold enough to call on Him. When he called on Jesus, a miracle of healing happened. Jesus restored his sight. You can receive something as well when you call on Jesus for mercy. Today, I pray that you get bold enough to call on Jesus for whatever you need in life. Do not let anyone get in the way. What was interesting is that Jesus told His disciples to bring Bartimaeus to Him. The scripture says: he immediately received his sight and followed Jesus (Mark 10:46-52). This means that Jesus heard his cry and answered Him. He will hear your cry. Because Jesus proves His love, you will be like Bartimaeus and follow Jesus. The power of His love will bless you and you will want to follow Him the rest of your life. God reminds us that prophecies, tongues and knowledge are all powerful, but they will never outlast love. It is the power of love that gives us hope and faith to believe that we will reign with Jesus forever. I Corinthians 13 in the King James Version speaks of love. It uses the word charity. Charity means love. **1 Corinthians 13:4-8 Charity suffereth long, and is kind; charity envieth not; charity vaunteth not itself, is not puffed up, Doth not behave itself unseemly, seeketh not her own, is not easily provoked, thinketh no evil; Rejoiceth not in iniquity, but rejoiceth in the truth; Beareth all things, believeth all things, hopeth all things, endureth all things. Charity never faileth: but whether there be prophecies, they shall fail; whether there be tongues, they shall cease; whether there be knowledge, it shall vanish away.**

Questions:

What does 1 Corinthians 13 tell us love is?_____
_____
_____
_____

List what love never does._____
_____
_____

CHAPTER 14

CHURCH IS THE TREATMENT CENTER GOD'S HOUSE

Matthew 16:16-18 And Simon Peter answered and said, Thou art the Christ, the Son of the living God. And Jesus answered and said unto him, Blessed art thou, Simon Barjona: for flesh and blood hath not revealed it unto thee, but my Father which is in heaven. And I say also unto thee, That thou art Peter, and upon this rock I will build my church; and the gates of hell shall not prevail against it.

When I first realized the work my Father did, as we were growing up, I had a strong respect for him. His job was constructing beautiful high-end homes in wealthy neighborhoods. Wow! My father did this kind of work for over 40 years. It was his love for family that kept him working through extreme adverse weather conditions. On some of the coldest days my father was at work to support his family. Inspired by my father's work throughout the years, I would later go to college thinking that I would become an architect or builder. I went to school to major in construction management until my eyes opened to my true calling! I am blessed because of God and my father!

Aside from the architectural drawings and building a small model home in my college class, I learned a lot. I learned that every home has a foundation, in which a slab exists below to support everything else. Below the slabs are footings that support the slab and the entire foundation. Footings consist of concrete and reinforcement bars placed inside of a trench below the slab. It's used especially in soil that is weak. Everything is built up from that slab-basic foundation. Nothing will destroy that foundation because of the strength in it and the way it's positioned.

My biological Father, Joe Arthur Doyle, left a permanent and inspirational impression in my mind, heart, spirit and soul as he raised me and my siblings to work for a living and be the best at what we do. All it took was my father's intervention in my life to get me started. My father will always be my hero because of the way he lived and blessed his family! My father took care of us. I would not have had any success if it were not for my father being a real genuine man of God. Love remains maxed out through my parents as they raised us to be a close family. Yes, their love sparked us to have family reunions after they had passed away. The love for my parent's lives eternally in my heart! I know I will see them again, one day by the power of Jesus Christ my Lord.

Our Lord wants us to know so much in this passage (Matthew 16:16-18). Two quick points capture our attention. Jesus tells Peter who Peter is to be. He is a church leader assigned by God. The second point is that Jesus tells Peter that His Father revealed Jesus's identity to Peter. Jesus does the same thing in identifying Peter. Think about what kind of heart Peter had to have to receive Jesus identity from the Father in Heaven. Jesus called Peter, blessed. He is blessed because he has been given answers directly from heaven that Jesus is God's Son. Jesus gives Peter a new name. The Greek word Petros is given to Peter for his firmness and steadfastness and it translates as rock. Both words are different, Petros is masculine and means a small rock or piece of rock; Petra is feminine, and it means the bedrock or a massive rock formation. It's important to understand that Jesus is only speaking to Peter, not other Apostles or Christians (Matthew 16).

Love maxed out is when Jesus gives you the power of protection and blessings from His church so that the gates of hell will not prevail against you. Love maxed out is when Jesus enters your heart! Love max out is when Jesus gives you all the promises in scripture! It is also the death, burial and resurrection of Jesus for your life! It is the blood of Jesus that covers you every day of your life.

CHURCH IS THE TREATMENT CENTER (PT1)

Love is the center focus of everything for God. The treatment center exists, and God has all the authority over it! The primary reason for this passage is because the gates of hell will never prevail because Jesus already has the victory. Jesus took the keys. The enemy does not have access to your heart when you are born again. Jesus is the rock! The writer says upon this rock, I will build my church and the gates of hell shall not prevail. The church has continuous power. The church is filled with love. Jesus is the head of the church (1 Colossians 1). This is the kind of topic that needs to be preached around the world to numerous people. The church is a treatment center where the Jesus is the Chief Physician. He is our healer. He is the restorer to bring His people back to spiritual health.

The church is the place where you can find and discover all treatments for any issue. Get into the house of the Lord where He dwells! Ask Him to live inside your heart. You need treatment today! You need Him to get inside of you now! Please understand that nothing is impossible for God. God does things according to

His will and word. He is not on our timeline. He is on His timeline in which no one knows. God is never late. When you call Him, He hears you and will answer. God is looking for saints with an obedient spirit. He is looking for those that are lost as well. You know if you are lost, don't you? If not, here is a big hint! You never go to church or spend time worshipping Him. You don't pray. God's treatment center can turn you around. You will praise and worship the Living God. The grips of hell must release you. The treatment center will stop the enemy from pulling you down.

One of the biggest misconceptions is that people think anybody who joins and/or performs in the church is automatically of the household of faith. God certainly loves you, however, you must be born again and be a true and faithful believer. Some also misunderstands the way the church is supposed to operate. The church must operate under God's divine power. No matter what anyone does, God will still have His way in the church.

Many younger people are at odds with the church because they have their own hang ups and personal let downs. There is always a time and chance that you can change your routine and your way of thinking and get involved for real. You can be a real worshiper. Specifically, younger people have some of the biggest opportunities to shine in the house of God. Too many allow Satan to cast a negative perception of the church in their minds.

I was watching Hillsong (a huge ministry) on television. They were worshiping God in a mighty way! Their team was comprised of various age groups, young and older. God has a place for every person on this earth to praise and worship Him. It was a blessing to see. Young people want to be treated like they are important and have talent. Treating a person with love and kindness inside the treatment center (church) has a huge impact on all groups and cultures. Positive treatment is the key to all ministries moving in the direction to glorify God. Treat people with dignity and respect in the church and you will produce a warrior on fire for God. I also saw the zeal and talent people displayed on other television programs. One key thing I concluded that allowing young people to perform on stage is a way to recruit them and get them started in that specific talent, hopefully that will motivate them to ask God for gifts in the ministry. There are nine ministry gifts listed in 1 Corinthians 12 that God wants to give to you. Ask Him and believe. Read (1 Samuel 16:7).

Questions and Discussions:

What does this verse mean to you Matthew 16? _____
_____
_____

What is the key focus in Matthew 16? _____
_____
_____

What does Peter mean in Matthew 16? _____
_____
_____

What makes the church a treatment center? _____

_____

What would like to be treated for? _____
_____
_____

Will you witness to friends about the church as a treatment center? _____

What healing scriptures best support the treatment center?

_____
_____

CHURCH IS THE TREATMENT CENTER (PT2)

Jeremiah 30:17 But I will restore you to health and heal your wounds, declares the Lord, because you are called an outcast, Zion for whom no one cares. Psalm 147:3 He heals the brokenhearted and binds up their wounds.

God's church has people from all backgrounds and personalities. The key to winning them is to invite and show love! We should always make people feel comfortable and at peace. There are haters, idolaters, drug addicts, bullies, prostitutes, pimps, ex-cons, adulterers, fornicators, lovers of men and women (Galatians 5:16-22 and Romans 1) who attend church from time to time. When people show up and are open to Him, Jesus will release His word, and show forth his power through deliverance, healing, and miracles. He is in the church. He is present in our worship services and is always ready make a change in your life and mine.

The Holy Spirit shows up to touch your family and deliver blessings in your life! Start showing up every Sunday to praise and worship Him. Come to the House of God and receive the living word of God for your life and your family's. The Lord is working on all of us. Not one person on the planet has arrived in perfection. Come and get your healing, deliverance and blessings.

There are many people that need prayer to get the Savior into their lives. Pray that God answers your request to be restored. Pray that God puts in you the right mindset, the right spirit and a clean heart. Only God can change all these areas. Are you ready for a treatment from the mighty hands of God? He is the Great Physician. You can pray for deliverance right now! Get rid of pride! Get Jesus in your life! One visit to the church can be a life changingexperience. He will deliver and heal you, and your loved ones. Jesus comes to strengthen the church! God is true and faithful to His word. Others will let you down! But Jesus will never let you down. This does not mean He will give you everything you want. He knows what is best for you.

Jesus is also no respect of person. No one has the power to judge you or put you out of God's church! The biggest focus of the church is love, and your entry to heaven. All your treatment comes from God and it's with love. Be reminded that everything is according to His will and purpose. He can restore all people. Count on it! Who in their right mind would want to miss out on God's blessings? The church is also referred to as purpose being a hospital, waiting for more patients to arrive. You can come any day. Don't miss Sunday worship service because you have a hang up with someone. You are clearly under attack, if that is the case.

It would be great also if people could start viewing this treatment center as a place to worship. Worship and praise is God's highest priority. Love has everything to do with it. When we show love it's a powerful thing. When we fail to even smile at a person, it gives a negative impression. It shouldn't be hard to smile when God continues to bless your life. Let's not give the devil an inch. God wants us to stand tall in the treatment center. Don't treat anyone like they are invisible. Everyone is important in God's kingdom. Don't treat them with a hardened heart. God has the power to change a hardened heart. The same God changed Pharaoh. God spoke in Jeremiah that he could take away the stony heart. The treatment center is for all to experience change. No matter what their sin, people want to be treated with dignity. When you come into the church, shake someone's hand, speak kind words, and lift them up with a smile. Invite them to come back. Let them know it was nice meeting them and their families. Always make people feel welcome and not like you are examining them. Tell them more about Jesus. Tell how he blesses your family. Share how God heard your cry! In 2 Chronicles 7:14 if my people, who are called by my name, will humble themselves and pray and seek my face and turn from their wicked ways, then I will hear from heaven, and I will forgive their sin and will heal their land.

The church is the treatment center. Jesus performed a great deal of healing in His ministry to show us His example of what the church should be doing. I love the fact that in Matthew 9:1-8, Jesus heals a paralyzed man who had been in his condition for 38 years. In the treatment center, called the church, you can meet Jesus. Jesus will remove your paralyzed condition of drugs, hate, pain, divorce, adultery, fornication and all the other sins. Jesus will bring you into the blessed life. Read Psalm 103 completely because it will change you. It has done some work in my body, soul, and spirit. No more excuses as if someone skipped over you. Don't miss this opportunity to get Jesus. For thirty-eight years the paralyzed man was making excuses that no one would help him. Jesus healed him so fast, it blew his mind. Hopefully, you will never turn your back on Jesus again. You will want to serve Him and become a witness to His grace and mercy. What is it that you need from Jesus? Ask and you will receive, if you believe (Matthew 9). Jesus also said this in Luke 4 and it's in Isaiah 61:1, The Spirit of the Sovereign Lord is on me, because the Lord has anointed me to proclaim good news to the poor. He has sent me to bind up the brokenhearted, to proclaim freedom for the captives and release from darkness for the prisoners

A simple faith-filled prayer can get rid of all your troubles. Jesus is the Great Physician and He can treat you for anything if you believe on Him and it's His will. Inside the treatment center-church, the Physician can drive demons away. He can equip you to evangelize and serve. The Great Physician can fix your attitude and behavior problems. Jesus can also repair sexual and immoral problems that don't line up with His word. (Romans 1:18-22.) Jesus can do miracles. You can be born again, transformed, and sanctified (John 3:3). You can receive salvation through Jesus and His word Romans 10:9. You can prepare for that great day of being caught up in the air - rapture (1 Thessalonian 4:16-18).

THE POWER OF LOVE

1 Corinthians 13:13 And now these three remain: faith, hope and love. But the greatest of these is love.

After Pearl Harbor was attacked on December 7, 1941 on a naval base at Oahu Island, Hawaii and thousands of United States soldiers were killed due to this surprise attack by Japan. The enemy hit our land with surprise and power! This started World War II. President Harry Truman decided to unleash two atomic bombs as revenge for Japan's attack on the United States. This should have been no surprise to the people of Japan. In August of 1945, during the final stages of the World War, the United States dropped atomic bombs on Japanese cities of Hiroshima and Nagasaki. These two atomic bombs killed an estimated 129,000 people. It had been perhaps the only use of nuclear weapons for warfare. This war changed the world. Can you image the amount of power inside those bombs? There was no escaping the power and effects of these bombs. These bombs have power, but they still do not exceed God's power. The force of those bombs do not compare to the force of God's love.

The Civil War of 1861 to 1865 was also a tragedy where the enemy, caused a divided country to kill each other over slavery and state rights. War is deadly, and it needs to come to an end once and for all. The evil one uses his power to cause war. God made us to live in peace and harmony. The only power that defeats war is the power of God. Every nation must turn to God and worship Him alone.

Everyone must turn to the greatest power which is love from God. Today's world concentrates on the super power. This means a country that has the most powerful means of warfare over other countries can dominate. You need to know there is no one on the planet or anything in existence that can escape the power of love. Because God is love. Love is more powerful than war. In fact, love is the key in overcoming war.

The meaning of love in the Webster dictionary is an intense feeling of deep affection. Another definition states as being a deep romantic and sexual attachment. In the Bible, it's called agape love which means it's unconditional. You don't earn God's love. He just gives love because of who He is. Love is the primary power that sustains us by our Lord, Jesus Christ. We are unable to live without love. Love sustains all humanity. Humans are a direct reflection of God's love. Love is the very fabric of our being. Everyone needs love! Love creates an attachment from a psychological standpoint. It is far greater from God's standpoint. For example, if a baby is without the mother, you will hear a cry that might shake the ground and reach your ear drums. This simply means that a bond between mother and baby is very strong and there is automatically a need for both mother and child. The attachment goes basically both ways. If you take the baby from the mother, she can become a raging female lion with dangerous emotions, capable of causing serious damage. The baby cries until you get the right nurturer to that baby. This reflects serious love. God expressed it in marriage and the first family. Love is more important than eating and drinking. Love is a requirement for all God's people as well. Jesus sent his disciples out to save souls in Luke 9. In John 15, He expects His disciples to bear fruit and be connected to Jesus. Without love, hatred and bitterness will take root and devour your spirit man. Without love, you can't bear fruit. In fact, without love, you are extremely broken. Ask Jesus to come in! Tell Him that you are desperate for His love. If you do not have a relationship with Jesus, then the devil and his demons will take up residence in your life. They will devour you and start working on each member in your household (Mark 5). Please tell Jesus that you want your household saved. Do you remember when the rich man wanted someone to go back and tell his brothers to get their lives together (Luke 16). Love will help you get your house in order. Love will help you tell all your family members about Jesus and the salvation He offers freely. When a brother is on his sick bed, there is a love that kicks in overdrive to go and help him. Love is thicker than water! Love has power that surpasses all things! The best help you can give is prayer. The Lord healed my brother from two lung surgeries and cancer. I know the supernatural works of God. I know miracles are real in Jesus name. I am so grateful to the Lord for his love poured out on my brother's life.

Love will help you clean out your house. It may be painful, but you will know that true love is in your home. More importantly, love has the greatest power because of the finished work of Jesus Christ, the Son of the living God. Love is the remedy for anything. Love can cure the world because God is the cure! Every time someone is healed, it's the power of God's love in action.

Someone once said that Bob Marley, a famous Jamaican reggae singer and song writer believed that music sends off the power of love that heals. In 1976, he performed in a free concert and was wounded in the chest and arm by an unknown shooter. Some thought the concert was over. He proceeded two days later with the concert. Some asked him, why. His response was that people that are trying to make the world worse are not taking a day off. So why should I? What an attitude to show love. God will use people in His own way to make a difference in this world. Jesus already showed us that love does cure people. Every mission that Jesus went on was to express the power heal through love. Are you going to take a day off or get to work? Jesus did not take a day off when His father sent Him to show love. He went about His Father's business showing the power of love. He died on a cross and paid the ransom for my sin with His love. He took away everything unclean in me and washed me whiter than snow! Isaiah 53:5 says "But he was wounded for our transgressions, he was bruised for our iniquities: the chastisement of our peace was upon him; and with his stripes we are healed." Every stripe on His body caused by the Roman's whip was a love mark for sinners. He took on all the wrath for you and me! Every stripe represents forgiveness, mercy, and grace. His blood washes us whiter than snow. I exalt you Lord Jesus!

LOVE FILLS VOID PLACES INSIDE YOU

Colossians 2:10 and in Him you have been made complete, and He is the head over all rule and authority.

Sabrina had longed for Kevin to be her husband for many years. They had been living in the same neighborhood and going out on dates. Kevin had a change of heart. His heart was on another person that he had met in college. He had been spending late nights elsewhere after college classes were over. Sabrina thought nothing of it because she felt secure in His arms and love. She felt complete with Kevin. When Kevin left her for another woman, she felt empty inside and believed that she could never love another. She finally met someone special about eight months later. She met Jesus while she was on the job. He changed her life and filled the empty places of her heart. Now Sabrina is a worshiper. She spends her time studying the word of God and praising Him!

There are times in life that people have desires that are unfulfilled. You do need to understand that He knows your need. He is the only one who can complete you! You may thirst for something, but you need God to quench that thirst. Listen to what the scripture says, In Jesus you have been made complete. This is for born-again people. A Christian should not walk around acting defeated. Everything we lack is in Jesus Christ. He is the only one who fulfills desires. God always reminds us of His word. Jesus tells us in Colossians 2:10 "And you have been filled by him, who is the head of every ruler and authority." You can always find yourself in Jesus Christ. We can have many void places in our lives and in the heart when Jesus is not present. At times, the enemy will try to trick us as Christians to make us believe that God is not in your heart. In John 10:10 Jesus tells us " The thief comes only to steal and kill and destroy; I came that they may have life, and have it abundantly." It's always an attack on our minds when something else outside of God is trying to depress us and hold us down. Many times, it's because we're looking for something in the flesh or some human to bless us, please us and fill the hollow places in our hearts. When you feel that hole opening inside your heart, call on Jesus name and ask the Holy Spirit to fill that place of loneliness and all needs. Speak victory over yourself. God is good in your life. Speak the word and know that you are not empty and that there is nothing lacking inside of you. Don't get depressed or defeated. Don't feel sad or suicidal. Jesus is already on your side and He will fill you and make you whole! Depression may come up against you. You just have to speak strength and blessings into your life in Jesus name.

When you feel like the world is against you and no one loves you, understand that Jesus loves you even more. He never leaves you!!The Bible is so clear when it says, I will never leave you, nor forsake you. You are never abandoned! He fills every place in your mind, heart, soul and spirit. God is good all the time. You just need to be reminded that the enemy plays tricks on the mind. Don't let him in. Don't give him an inch! You won't have those void places anymore once you have Jesus in your heart. As a Christian, you are constantly being filled by the Holy Spirit, daily

(Ephesians 5:18). You need to have faith that God's power is working inside of you, right now. You also need to be reminded that when you are born again, you are a member of Jesus' family. (John 3:3). That is the answer. Being born again mean Jesus is inside your heart and you are baptized in the Father, Son and Holy Ghost. Your life is changed forever. You are a new creature. You are a child of the King of glory. Give God praise and glory. You now have someone you can always depend. **Remember these verses: Ephesians 4:13 says until we all attain to the unity of the faith, and of the knowledge of the Son of God, to a mature man, to the measure of the stature which belongs to the fullness of Christ." Psalm 81:10 says "I, the LORD, am your God, who brought you up from the land of Egypt; Open your mouth wide and I will fill it."**

CHAPTER 15

TAKE YOUR LIFE BACK

MATTHEW 17:19-20 Then came the disciples to Jesus apart, and said, Why could not we cast him out? And Jesus said unto them, Because of your unbelief: for verily I say unto you, If ye have faith as a grain of mustard seed, ye shall say unto this mountain, Remove hence to yonder place; and it shall remove; and nothing shall be impossible unto you.

If you love God enough, you will take your life back! If you are not a Christian, your first step in taking your life back is surrendering your life to Jesus Christ. In Romans 10:9 it says accept Jesus as your Lord and Savior. He will come into your heart and make you new again. All your answers for life are in the Bible! Jesus did not give you life abundantly so that you could let your life go off path! Wake up, get up and strengthen yourself in the Lord! Give the devil notice! God did not give you the spirit of fear, but of power, love and a sound mind (2 Timothy 1:7). So, go right ahead and rebuke that demon and speak the word as you chase it out of your house, in Jesus's name. Jesus rebuked the demon inside of a boy in Matthew 17:14-20. He called out that demon (who was manifesting in the form of seizures and suffering) and the boy was healed at that very moment. Then Jesus told his disciples that they had so little faith. If you have faith the size of a mustard seed, you can move mountains and take your life back. The key is to have that kind of faith in Jesus's power! God never asked you to accept all those mountains in your life. Those mountains represent things that steal your joy and drain the life out of you. That is the work of Satan and his demons. Take your life back because God gave it to you. Your life never should have been taken in the first place. When the enemy causes you to lose your focus on your life, he is trying to make void places inside of you. Why? The enemy desires to fill your spirit with his demonic spirit. Matthew 12:43-45 says "When an impure spirit comes out of a person, it goes through arid places seeking rest and does not find it. Then it says, I will return to the house I left. When it arrives, it finds the house unoccupied, swept clean and put in order. Then it goes and takes with it seven other spirits more wicked than itself, and they go in and live there. And the final condition of that person is worse than the first. That is how it will be with this wicked generation." God wants all of us to look to Jesus our deliverer! Cast all your cares on Him!

The only person that wants to steal your life is Satan. Yes, he is like a roaring lion seeking to rip us apart. The Bible says "Be sober, be vigilant; because your adversary the devil, as a roaring lion, walketh about, seeking whom he may devour (1 Peter 5:8)." Today you need to make up your mind that you are taking your life back now! Take your life back from things that control you. Take your life back from pornography. Take your life back from things that obsess you. Take your life back from idol worship and from everything that holds you back. You take your life back by not just speaking but through action and reading the word of God. James 5. Be doers of the word. Take action by reading and praying in the spirit and in the word of God will also fill those empty areas in your life. The word of God is supernatural. It works miracles. Meditate on the word, pray and take action. Take steps that deliver you out of all of bondages. Get into a spiritual routine.

Sign up for weekly events at the church and in your community. You could even start a prayer cell that meets in certain locations to pray several days a week. You can also do Bible study every week in your home and at church. You can also get into a fitness routine. You can also practice memorizing scripture passages as well with a friend or family member. You can also go to a park and museums and out to restaurants and dine. You can also be creative for your church and create programs that will enhance church ministries. If you just sit still all the time, then you may feel empty inside. So, get busy! Be a servant in God's kingdom!

Questions and Discussion:

1. What is your first step in taking your life back? _____
_____

2. How do you overcome feelings of depression?
_____
_____

3. How do you fill the voids inside of you? _____
_____
_____

4. What role does Jesus play in your life? _____
_____
_____

5. What makes you sure that you are born again?

_____

_____

6. What will you do to take your life back? List seven things:

_____

_____

_____

IT'S ABOUT RELATIONSHIPS

Most people struggle at taking their lives back because they don't have a relationship with Jesus Christ. You simply can't live on earth without one. It is through means of a relationship that we function coherently a relationship with Jesus. Live with the power of love. If you are having difficulty with relationships, assess your relationship with the Lord. Love resides in relationship.

Your primary relationship should be with Jesus Christ as your Lord and Savior. Although we all know that your first bonding relationship is primarily with your mother and your father. However, you must seek a relationship with Jesus Christ. You must ask him to enter your heart. If you want your relationships to be in the top condition, follow the steps below.

Examine your personal relationships in these areas:

Step 1. You must have a relationship with Christ Jesus. Do you know for sure that you have salvation (Romans 10:9)?

Step 2. Know the person with whom you have a relationship. Know It because there are several different kinds of relationships.

Step 3. Through prayer and discernment, you can determine if this is the right relationship. Create methods to make it work better.

Step 4. Examine your heart daily through prayer and scripture reading to nurture and improve your relationship.

Step 5. Have a prayer life to Jesus as your Lord and Savior. Involve the person in relationship with you. Remember you need to be equally yoked.

Step 6. Develop goals in marriage to improve the relationships. Make your marriage fun! Laughter is good for the heart!

Step 7. Maintain the relationship daily by providing love (1Corinthians 13).

Step 8. If something is broken in the relationship restore one another with love and kindness and gentleness.

Step 9. Speak up regarding your relationship for love and survival in your relationship.

Step 10. Love is just as essential as nutrients, blood and oxygen to your body. We all need love!

Step 11. Never let anything come between your relationships. Stand for the truth and trust your partner.

Step 12. If married the scripture says that you are one (Mark

10:8-10). Nothing should ever tear you apart

Step 13. Make proper corrections in relationships with your children. Correct them and train them in love (Proverbs 22).

Step 14. Do not allow money to dictate your life nor take your relationships off of course (1 Timothy 6:10).

Step 15. Making proper decisions and adequate corrections staying on path in Jesus Christ (1 Timothy 3:16).

Step 16. Break out of any habits that are toxic which can lead to a catastrophic interrupting life and relationships.

Step 17. Repeat them if needed.

CHAPTER 16

MOSES: THE MAN OF GOD

Numbers 12:1-10 Miriam and Aaron began to talk against Moses because of his Cushite wife, for he had married a Cushite. "Has the Lord spoken only through Moses?" they asked. "Hasn't he also spoken through us?" And the Lord heard this. Now Moses was a very humble man, humbler than anyone else on the face of the earth. At once the Lord said to Moses, Aaron, and Miriam, "Come out to the tent of meeting, all three of you." So, the three of them went out. Then the Lord came down in a pillar of cloud; he stood at the entrance to the tent and summoned Aaron and Miriam. When the two of them stepped forward, he said, "Listen to my words: "When there is a prophet among you, I, the Lord, reveal myself to them in visions, I speak to them in dreams. But this is not true of my servant Moses; he is faithful in all my house. With him I speak face to face, clearly and not in riddles; he sees the form of the Lord. Why then were you not afraid to speak against my servant Moses?" The anger of the Lord burned against them, and he left them. When the cloud lifted from above the tent, Miriam's skin was leprous —it became as white as snow. Aaron turned toward her and saw that she had a defiling skin disease, and he said to Moses, "Please, my lord, I ask you not to hold against us the sin we have so foolishly committed.

Moses was God's leading man. The reason God was so pleased with Moses is because Moses was more faithful than all of God's people and humbler than any one on the face of the earth. Moses had a relationship with God that boggles the human mind. I had already seen the movie, The Ten Commandments; however, Sunday night at midnight a movie came on about Moses leading God's people through the desert. One thing, I have learned in this story of Moses is that God loved Moses. I had already seen on many occasions that Moses demonstrated his love to God by obeying Him as he visited Pharaoh on several occasions, telling him to let God's people go. Moses was God's man of deliverance! Moses was indeed a man of God filled with God's anointing, power, love, and compassion. He was a chosen deliverer sent by God to Egypt to tell Pharaoh to free God's people. Moses was humble, meek and obedient to God. When Moses spoke, it was from his heart directly from God. I saw the relationship Moses had with God on several occasions in those scenes. It moved me in a new way of ministry and listening to the Holy Spirit. I also remember in several scenes, Moses kept telling people that God talks to him and him to God.

Even after God forgave Aaron for his disobedience and idolatry for creating a golden calf, God still allowed Aaron to be a priest from the tribe of Levites. I saw something else. It was the compassion and love Moses had for His brother to continue in the priesthood after God had forgiven him. Moses covered these people and they knew it. They followed Moses because they knew Moses had a relationship with God and was anointed by God; and they needed deliverance in so many ways. Their deliverance was about to happen. The authority God gave Moses surpassed just about anything we could imagine. When Moses presented those Ten Commandments, they stored them in the ark of covenant. It pleased God. Moses' authority from God covered the priesthood and all the people of Israel. God even blessed Joshua later through Moses. Moses was so loving and filled with compassion. God struck Miriam with leprosy for mouthing off and being disrespectful to Moses, making him upset. God saw it and she had to pay a price. Moses still took care of her, even though she was to be an outcast for several days.

The Bible is clear! The word of God tells us not to touch God's anointed and do his prophets no harm (Psalm 105:15). This also means keep your mouth off them. If Miriam was here, she would tell you the same. Moses later transferred authority and leadership to Joshua. God used Moses to give Joshua blessings, acknowledging that Joshua was God's choice. Moses moved them to see the Promised Land and Joshua took them into it. God has a love that man can never understand. Nevertheless, God wants us to just receive His love. God is so good and merciful; He still blessed a murmuring people because of Moses. It's amazing that God sent an anointed man of God their way and some just didn't believe. When they experience what Miriam, Aaron and the people Moses delivered from Egypt experience their heart will open to God. Sometimes it takes some tough love to convince people of who God is.

LOVE ABIDES

JOHN 15:7 "If you abide in me, and My words abide in you, you will ask what you desire, and it shall be done for you.

Harvey Reynolds had joined a religious group and they had welcomed him with open arms and immediately made him feel important. They put him in a high position to manage all the other spies they had in other organizations. It took a little while for

Harvey to see through the facade and lies of this religion organization. They had millions of dollars contributed by actors in Hollywood who had also been deceived and brain washed. Harvey was accused of stealing funds as an excuse to get rid of him. By that time, Harvey had adapted and had become slightly brain washed.

If you remain in something and have a strong belief in it, your mind and heart can be vested in it. You can become blind. One huge problem is that this religion was not of God. It has all the wrappings and appearance, but it is not of God. Jesus tells us to try the spirit and see if they are from God. Many false prophets have gone into the world (1 John 4:1). When a friend of Harvey came back from Iraq and visited Harvey, he discovered something new by talking to Jason Myles. Jason had lost about 8 buddies in combat and before he left Iraq, he had gotten into a prayer group on open opportunities and accepted Jesus as Lord. In some of the study groups, he learned the scripture. He was the one who rescued Harvey from the cult. Harvey now pastors at one the largest ministries in America, where souls are saved every Sunday. God can pull you out of things. You should praise Him and give Him glory. The reason Jason could convince Harvey is because Jason was abiding in Jesus. His relationship had deepened to the point that he knew it was time to bear fruit in Jesus name.

The lesson is to think on Jesus for inspiration. Secondly, if you are in a ministry and it does not feel right in the spirit or any kind of way, get out of it. Do not remain in that religion! It is obviously not of God! You already know better! Run! Can you imagine all those people with blinders on and living under the impressions of false prophets, like David Karesh and Jim Jones? This is real! False religions and false prophets will try to take over your life. There are cults everywhere, do not get involved with them. They are satanic and will destroy your life and family. Be careful because some disguise themselves in various forms. The word of God does not abide in any of those people. They use tricks and manipulation and have controlling spirits (demonic). They (false prophets) sound good to those listening. You need to know the word for yourself. Start studying the word daily.

If you are a follower of Jesus Christ, love abides in you. To abide in Him simply means to remain in Him. This is a powerful word because it means stay in the same place where God points you. At the same time, reject any spirit that is antichrist. You must test the spirit (1 John 4:1). Do not let any religion (such as Muslim, Hinduism, Islam, Buddhism, Kistna, scientology, or any other) influence you in any way to leave Jesus Christ. The blessed hope is in Jesus Christ, our lord. If you are really one of Jesus's children, the Bible declares that nothing can pluck you out of His hand. Remain in Jesus. Power is in His name. When you are in His presence a breakthrough can happen. It is Jesus who will help you to recover from all attacks. Even when storms and floods come, Jesus is on your side. Once you have tasted sweet Jesus, you will never go back. Because you are a believer and have received salvation, you are a kingdom child of God. You are a family member in God's kingdom. Your life is to remain in Him who brought you out of darkness to His marvelous light. Once you abide in Jesus, you are connected to the best and most powerful love source in existence. Nothing else is comparable. Jesus wants all believers to remain in Him to be fruitful. You don't remain in him without doing any works. Start bearing fruit and don't you let anything make you fall away (John 15:1-10).

Marriage is one of the most powerful institutions God wants

us to remain in (Mark 10:7-8). It's a blessed relationship. Even in your marriage you must bear fruit. It takes two to make love work in that relationship.

There was one woman in the church who was easily enticed to start back on the club scene. She was listening to rock and roll, rhythm and blues, and attending concerts where just about anything goes. This caused a problem in her relationship with her husband because he wanted to concentrate on Jesus. She manipulated him and conned him which made him fall from the faith. Some people call it witchcraft, a Jezebel spirit was used to entice and persuade her husband. The point is that none of this behavior is love. Love encourages the husband to stand for Jesus. It is good to have a wife that sees the slightest disappointment or something that distracts or affect the husband, she reminds him to just serve Jesus.

Thank God for a woman that will constantly stand out front, praising and worshipping God. That's the kind of wife a brother needs. He needs someone to love and protect him from all those witchcraft and manipulation spirits. Sam's wife did not understand that she was betraying her husband and destroying him spiritually, all to have her selfish way. The point is when you do not abide in Jesus, you are abiding in something else, and usually it's a demon (Mark 5) (John 15).

In Psalm 37:4, He said, "If you delight yourself in Him, He will give you the desires of your heart." Ask Jesus to help you to abide in Him in your Christian walk so you can please God and help someone else.

Questions & Discussion:

What does abiding mean to you in John 15? _____

_____
_____

Write 3 things about John 15 that applies to you_____

_____
_____
_____

Are you abiding in Jesus Christ now? _____

Are you a fruitful Christian? _____

SPIRIT CLASH

DROP ALL BULLIES IN JESUS NAME

When people clash, it is sometimes due to an evil bullying spirit. Nobody is playing around with bullies. Ask God to help you stay out of physical confrontation. Although it may be hard. The spirit clash is simple. It is one person truly born again and the other person lost and led by the devil. The only bullies in life are led by an evil spirit. **1 JOHN 4:1-4 "Beloved, believe not every spirit, but try the spirits whether they are of God: because many false prophets are gone out into the world.**

Hereby know ye the Spirit of God: Every spirit that confesseth that Jesus Christ is come in the flesh is of God: And every spirit that confesseth not that Jesus Christ is come in the flesh is not of God: and this is that spirit of antichrist, whereof ye have heard that it should come; and even now already is it in the world. Ye are of God, little children, and have overcome them: because greater is he that is in you, than he that is in the world."

Parents check your child to make sure they are neither bullying anyone nor getting bullied. The bully is no more than a demon spirit orchestrating fear, manipulation and terror. Do not be fooled, the enemy uses people to bully. Sadly, the bully can't tell until one tough Christian stands up and fights back. Believe it or not bullying is in the church, school and some homes. Be ready to stand up to any bully!

I remember a time I changed my route to avoid some bullies in my neighborhood. Even though I was tough and would fight anybody with my bad temper, I still wanted to avoid conflict. Bullies existed then and now. At one point, we had a few bullies that I just hated and dreamed about beating them down. I just wanted someone to knock the bully out! In fact, I took a different route to school once before to avoid a confrontation with a bully. In my neighborhood, fights always broke out. I always had a quick fuse. I was a hot-tempered person growing up. I still thought me, and my brothers were fast like the golden boy, "Sugar Ray." Nevertheless, I still experienced bullies and did not think of it until I grew up. When you are young and live in a hood environment, some things you just don't think about until you grow up. One day one of the bullies forced my hand. I had to fight him! What he did not know was that my confidence level in boxing and fighting was at a high level. Just because I was quiet, he took me for granted. I also did not fear him. That was an advantage for me! Sometimes bullies overlook your true toughness because they are so arrogant, prideful and evil! A bully think that he or she already has the victory, until you prove that you have the victory in Jesus Christ! The bully got what he deserved that day! I would have preferred to show love in a different way. But I was forced to toughen up, face my enemy and go into action. He got roughed up that day! Bullies have evil spirits. They clash with your spirit! Its better if you can walk away unharmed. It is also better if you can call the police or report to another authority. I did not have the opportunity to do so! There comes a time when you have to stand up for yourself!

The enemy is that bully that enters your home when you are not watching or sometimes in your face! Drop that bully on his face by the word of God! It's the enemy who causes spirit clashes to see if you will cave in and break up relationships/marriages and friendships. God did not make you to cave in to a bully. God did not give us a weak, broken spirit of fear. God did not make you to believe every spirit. It is the Holy Spirit that will give you discernment. He tells us in the word that you will know them if they confess that Jesus came in the flesh. That will be your answer.

In 2 Timothy 1:7 the Bible tells us "For God hath not given us the spirit of fear; but of power, and of love, and of a sound mind." We don't run away when we have a spirit clash or are challenged by the enemy (bully). We have power in Jesus Christ. His name alone has all power in it! We have God on our side. We walk with the whole armor of God. When spirits clash, love is challenged in the life of the believer. What is meant by clashing spirits is that, they don't agree. These clashes happen between coworker, spouses, and others. It should be immediately addressed. The spirit of love can overcome any clashing moments. Use love as the treatment to resolve hate and evil. The enemy dished it out to test you. Get over the clash and get in love with Jesus. You don't have time for trivial mess. Fix it by drawing people with love and kindness. Speak nice and kind words to others and you will draw them. The power of love conquers everything! How? Jesus is in it. He is love. If you ever experience bullies, call on Jesus to help you through the situation. You are not to fear anyone or anything! Be strong in the Lord and the power of His might. Put on the whole armor of God (Ephesians 6).

Questions:

Write three items down that you see in 2 Timothy 1:7

_____

_____

_____

How does this apply to you? Give two examples.

_____

_____

_____

_____

How can this help you daily? List two examples.

_____

_____

CHAPTER 17

NOTHING SEPARATES YOU FROM GOD'S LOVE

ROMANS 8:35-39 Who shall separate us from the love of Christ? Shall trouble or hardship or persecution or famine or nakedness or danger or sword? As it is written: "For your sake we face death all day long; we are considered as sheep to be slaughtered." No, in all these things we are more than conquerors through him who loved us. For I am convinced that neither death nor life, neither angels nor demons, neither the present nor the future, nor any powers, neither height nor depth, nor anything else in all creation, will be able to separate us from the love of God that is in Christ Jesus our Lord.

The Apostle imagined searching the universe, galaxies and all existence and could not come up with anything more powerful than the love of God. The writer tells us that he is convinced that nothing can separate us from God. The Apostle uses the most powerful list of areas in life and death to make his point. He imagines that he searched those things and could not find where they could separate God's love. Hands down, love is stronger than all those areas the Apostle listed and all things.

God's love is displayed in so many ways. Can you imagine

what went through the minds of astronauts when they went into outer space and saw the stars, moon and galaxies.

The first man in space was the Soviet cosmonaut Yuri Gagarin, who made a single orbit of the Earth on April 12, 1961. The United States also ventured into outer space. The first United States astronaut into space was Alan Shepard, who made a suborbital flight on May 5, 1961. This was followed by another suborbital flight by Gus Grissom, and by a three-orbit flight by John Glenn on February 20, 1962. It was a few years later in my elementary school, when I began to learn about astronauts and space. One thing I remember is that it was a challenge to get rockets to safely carry a man into outer space. God has power in His unlimited galaxies Outer space and the universe are limitless, so is God's love. It is the same limitless love of God that protects us from meteoroids, asteroids and black holes. Our God has given us a promise that our final frontier or destination is in heaven to reign and live with God eternally!

Whenever you are challenged with something that wants priority in your life over God or things that try to dominate your life, you need to rebuke it. Walk away from things that are not associated with God. He has all power, and nothing can separate us from His love. Do not listen to anyone speaking opposite. In the preceding verses 31-34, the Apostle Paul reminds us that we are more than conquerors in Jesus Christ. He states this fact because Jesus died on the cross and was raised from the dead by the glory of His Father, and now is at the right hand of the Father in heaven, making intercession on behalf of the saints. He defeated Satan, death, and the grave. Jesus is the conqueror. He wants us to know that we will face challenges that will try to hinder us. Some experiences will try to convince us that God has left us alone.

I thought about a woman I saw giving her testimony on national television. This woman had no arms and much of her family had given up on her. The amazing thing is that she had a baby, but no help, except God. God gifted her by his power to change the baby diapers with her feet with precision. I thought about how grace and mercy shows up in Jesus name. Challenges of life can be cruel and rough. The enemy can show up to mess with your mind, but you must take authority. Take on any challenge God gives you and give Him glory. Don't let anyone make you quit. Don't listen to discouraging and negative spirits and family members. Don't quit on yourself or God! God will never leave you nor forsake you.

Nothing is better or powerful than God. The Apostle Paul concluded in that nothing can separate us from the love of God. There is nothing in existence to be measured against His love. I like this passage because it reminds me that even in death, His love covers all of us that are born again.

ROOTED IN JESUS CHRIST

Ephesians 3:17-19 that Christ may dwell in your hearts through faith; that you, being rooted and grounded in all love, may be able to comprehend with all the saints what is the width, the length and depth and height to know the love of Christ which passes knowledge; that you may be filled with all fullness of God.

A root is normally associated with plants and trees. It starts with a seed planted as the first step. The seed comes from God. In most cases, the root runs deep in the ground. Some roots are so strong that they run deep and back up onto surface. I was considering calling on a specialist to see if something could be done to stop the roots from spreading in my yard. The word of God is written for us to be rooted in the most power person in our lives, Jesus Christ. Every time I walk in my back yard, I see several huge trees that we planted. The things that always capture my attention are the roots that are in the ground because they are so huge and thick. You can tell that these roots are receiving nourishment. Therefore, the tree is alive and standing with strength. Psalms 1 tells us about being rooted by the rivers of the water to receive continuous nourishment that never ends. When you are rooted in Jesus, all power is accessible to you, in you and for you. However, you need the kind of faith that connects and anchors you to Jesus. Real faith is rooted in Christ. If a minister, deacon, or any church member falls from the faith because of some sin they should be rooted in Jesus enough to seek true repentance and get back into their proper position in Jesus Christ. You are connected to the fullness of God. Therefore, you are not to act, walk or look defeated. Hold your head up and call on Jesus in the time of need. Make no mistake you do need Him! You can act like you are so intellectual if you want, God will knock you to your knees or he will allow the devil to do it. All God has to do is remove his hand from your life or give the enemy permission to touch your life, then devastation will occur. One of the best examples in the Bible is the story of Job, a servant of God (Job 1). We need to have the kind of relationship Job had with God. We need to count our blessings. Ask Jesus to keep his hand on our lives.

What do you think the Apostle Paul was saying to the church?

Surely, he was encouraging them to know that the fullness of blessings is in our Lord, Jesus Christ. He was praying for the believers in the church at Ephesus that they would be strengthened in the inner man. He was encouraging them to hold on to Jesus Christ, who sanctifies, roots, and grounds us in the faith. You must be rooted and ground in Him to make it through the rough time of life. He knows that your heart is a vessel for His spirit to flow through and speak to for His purpose. Your faith is in Him.

Question and Discussion:

1. Are you rooted in Jesus? _____

2. What does being rooted mean to you? _____
_____
_____

3. What does it take for you to commit to being rooted in Jesus Christ? List 3
_____
_____
_____

4. Where should Jesus dwell according to Ephesians 3:17-19?
_____

CHAPTER 18

LOVE IN EVERY HEARTBEAT

Proverbs 4:23 Guard your heart above all else, for it determines the course of your life.

One movie I recall that had singers that moved the hearts of the crowd was called the Five Heartbeats. They used the lyrics call "a heart is a house for love" When the lead singer opened up with a loud opening pitch, he alone ignited the crowd as he held that note and then open with "Is there a heart in the house tonight? Stand up!" the woman on the front row fainted due to that opening song from one of the singers because it affected her heart! It's still in my mind how they lady's body sump down into her chair because of the power of music touched her heart. In spiritual world in Jesus Christ, our heart is a house for Jesus's spirit to dwell inside. We get fascinated with Christian Artist touching our hearts. It fascinates me to think on how good Jesus is in our lives. Then I think on why King David could not help but to sing praise to God in his Psalms listed in the Bible. Many artists have caught the fire of the word of God and use in gospel singing and groups are still multiplying. Kirk Franklin is one of those Gospel Artist that erupted on the scene and impacting millions even today. I was listening to his music on the road in 1994-96 as I travel to various military missions. One of Kirk Franklin's songs specifically was "Melodies from heaven rain down on me" I still love that song! But undoubtedly my favorite is "Hosanna" If there is anything that will touch a person's heart is music. It's like the heart is perfectly in tune to every beat of music and to every beat of the heart in some ways. The Holy Spirit knows how to connect music and melodies inside the heart.

Only God knows every beat of your heart throughout your life span. Just like everything else in life, love is inside your heart and every beat of your heart and it has a purpose. God gave so many things in His creation a heart and purpose. His people's hearts matter so much to Him. The right kind of heart pleases God. Pour your heart out in serving and worshiping God. God is always blessing us in the heart and in all areas of life. He even blessed us in every heartbeat. His spirit of love is in our hearts and every beat! In Proverbs 4:23 we are told to guard our heart above all else, it determines the course of life. In other words, keep Jesus in your heart to remain focused in the Christian life and against attacks of the adversary. In Ephesians 3:17, the Apostle Paul refers to your heart being rooted in Jesus Christ. Before you ever accepted Jesus as Lord and Savior and before you became rooted and grounded, Jesus already knew every beat of your hearts. What is a heartbeat? A heartbeat is the very life line of your life. If your heart stops beating, no life exists in you. Without blood flowing through your heart, the way God designed your heart, we would not be alive. We would not have any function in life. God is the scientist for your heart. Scientifically, the design of our heart points to the Heart Chambers, Valves, Vessels, Wall, and Conduction System. The heart is made up of four chambers. There are two upper chambers called atria and in single form its atrium and the lower two chambers are called the ventricles. Muscular walls, called septa or septum, divide the heart into two sides. Nevertheless, be advised this design came from God, the one we are to worship and give thanks to every day. God gave us a heart.

Why? God gave us a heart to live and to know Him through worship and service. If you want to confirm this fact, all you have to do is open your bible and look at everyone that served God in the Bible from the time of Adam (Genesis) to John in (Revelations). You will see Men, Women, young people and Angels serving God.

One of the most powerful things about the heart is that people can't see it and it works automatic in the spirit and flesh. The heart is at the center of life and contains the intellect, will, emotions and moral consciousness. The other powerful fact is that God knows and can see everything about each person's heart. In both Old and New Testaments, the heart is viewed as center of personality and spiritual life. Every chamber of the heart has God's love inside of it. The part you can't see is the spiritual element of the heart. God's spirit resides inside the heart of the believer. God has residence inside of you. Where you go, the spirit goes. God wants us to be spirit lead. Listen, love is so powerful that when you sing you want to call melodies from heaven to rain down on you! You want to send melodies back up to heaven to glorify God! God put so much love inside of our hearts that he constructed it to love Him back and sing melodies in the highest of worship and praise!

THE POWER OF LOVE

INFUSED INTO YOUR DNA-BLOOD!

1 John 1:7 But if we walk in the light, as he is in the light, we have fellowship one with another, and the blood of Jesus Christ

his Son cleanseth us from all sin.

We all know that blood and oxygen are key elements to living. It's in the air you breathe, in your lungs and in your blood. What you might not know is how oxygen gets into your blood and how the blood carries oxygen through your body.

Blood and Oxygen – How It Works

You breathe air in through your nose and mouth. It makes its way into your lungs and dissolves in the water lining of the alveoli. Oxygen then clings to red blood cells as they pass through the alveolar capillaries - now the oxygen is in the blood. Things that get into our blood stream impacts our lives. Often people don't even understand what is going on with them because they don't understand the power of God allowing our bodies to function in the way He created them to function. It is God that helps us to stay alive.

This process of oxygen in our blood illustrates God's power at work inside of the human body. We can be resuscitated when either dead or barely alive, spiritually and physically. When I was in basic training over 33 years ago, the first thing they taught us were the steps to apply to a casualty: Stop, look and listen and feel a victim lying on the ground. Obviously, you ask them if they are okay, after you ensure the area is safe. The point is to apply mouth to mouth resuscitation (bring someone back to life) using rescue breathing. Once they breathe on their own, you can stop the rescue breathing. You have helped this person to breathe on their own with their own oxygen. You are life saver!

What does the acronym DNA stand for? DNA stands for deoxyribonucleic acid, it is a self-replicating material present in nearly all living organisms as the main constituent of chromosomes. It is the carrier of genetic information. It is also the fundamental and distinctive characteristics or qualities of someone or something, especially when regarded as unchangeable. DNA was discovered in 1869 by Frederick Miescher. It is important to understand that love is 100% infused inside of each person's DNA because of the love of God. Adam was created with perfect DNA by God our creator. Love was already infused into our DNA when God created us. I get excited to think about the breath of life breathed into my nostrils by God. You and I are not the creators of DNA. God created your DNA. God's hands are in your DNA. God is the designer and the origin of all mankind. In fact, the truth be told, all of us have blood so much alike regardless of skin color, that it would blow each person's mind. That is enough to break the spirit of racism and the devil's back!

The reason for the likeness in blood regardless of race is because God created all people in his image and likeness (Genesis 3). We were created to love and not miss a beat in sharing love! Every family believes so strongly in their family's blood line. What do not understand is that your blood, African American (Black), White, Hispanic Americans and all people has blood that matches. I believe that scientifically blood is very similar. Think about blood types. People of different races can share the same blood type. Society has thousands of interracial couples and families existing throughout the world because they are color blind and allow love to lead the way. Please become color blind for love's sake! You can do it with the power of God's love.

We all have a blood type. Human blood is grouped into four types: A, B, AB, and O. Each letter refers to a kind of antigen, or protein, on the surface of red blood cells. For example, the surface of red blood cells in Type A blood has antigens known as A-antigens. Regardless of race, if you need a blood transfusion, you will receive it the same method or procedure of any other race. Your blood does not make you better than the next person. Whites, blacks and some Hispanics are hating and killing each other over skin color (race) because the devil has blinded their eyes. Are your eyes and spirit open to this problem in society? Can you see better how the devil has stirred this up between races? Question: Who told you that your skin color is superior to another person? There is only one answer to this question. The answer is Satan. The enemy has blinded the minds of those who believe they are superior. Only Jesus Christ is superior! Read Colossians Chapter 1. Today, you can break the curse if you are willing to truly receive Jesus in your heart and bring peace about with all nationalities. Each person can make a difference in bringing peace and love to everyone around them, regardless of color of skin. When Jesus gave us life, all men were created equal. The Blood of Jesus covers all people. We are now infused by the blood of the Lamb, Jesus Christ. His grace is given to all and his love is shed abroad by the power of the Holy Spirit. Whatever is holding you back and has filled you with hate, ask Jesus to take it away. He can come into your heart and make you a new creature. Ask Him to cover you with His blood. Confess it and believe that Jesus is Lord and Savior in your life. Confess and believe that He died for you and was raised from the dead that you might have life. I will speak that I am a blood carrier of Jesus Christ. I am covered in the blood of the Lamb! The power of His love is inside of me and my DNA. So, I can walk in victory and power of His love. 1 John 5:5-8 "And who can win this battle against the world? Only those who believe that Jesus is the Son of God. And Jesus Christ was revealed as God's Son by his baptism in water and by shedding his blood on the cross not by water only, but by water and blood. And the Spirit, who is truth, confirms it with his testimony. So, we have these three witnesses the Spirit, the water, and the blood and all three agree.

Matthew 26:28 For this is my blood of the new testament, which is shed for many for the remission of sins.

In 1 John 2:2 And he is the propitiation for our sins: and not for ours only, but also for the sins of the whole world. Revelation 1:5 And from Jesus Christ, [who is] the faithful witness, [and] the first begotten of the dead, and the prince of the kings of the earth. Unto him that loved us, and washed us from our sins in his own blood, In Revelation 12:11 "And they overcame him by the blood of the Lamb, and by the word of their testimony; and they loved not their lives unto the death." In Hebrews 9:14 "How much more shall the blood of Christ, who through the eternal Spirit offered himself without spot to God, purge your conscience from dead works to serve the living God?"

In Hebrews 10:19-22 "Having therefore, brethren, boldness to enter into the holiest by the blood of Jesus, By a new and living way, which he hath consecrated for us, through the veil, that is to say, his flesh; And having an high priest over the house of God; Let us draw near with a true heart in full assurance of faith, having our hearts sprinkled from an evil conscience, and our bodies washed with pure water."

YOUR BODY IS A TEMPLE -PART 2

1 Corinthians 6:19-20 Do you not know that your bodies are

temples of the Holy Spirit, who is in you, whom you have received from God? You are not your own; you were bought at a price. Therefore, honor God with your bodies.

The conflict with Darwinism and those who believe in his theory is simple. They keep on missing God's word which is above all human intellect. A person without the spirit of God does not understand the things of God. Godly things are simply foolish to that person (1 Corinthians 2:14). When people study Darwinism, they believe in him and his intellect instead of proof that God created everything, and Jesus really existed then and now. It's amazing how a person can be turned on by someone else's intellect. The book of Genesis is clear! Genesis 1:27 So God created man in his own image, in the image of God created he him; male and female created he them.

This would be the time to address evolution. Charles Darwin was a man who proposed a theory that man evolved from apes. He was responsible for this theory called the evolution of natural selection. He developed it in his book written in 1859 entitled "On the Origin of Species." His writing was oriented as to express the process in his belief by which organism evolved or changed over a specific time resulting in heritable physical and behavioral traits. The point is that by 1870 much of society had accepted his scientific results due to it being so compelling to the scientific community and the public. This amazing insult to God is that people accepted Darwin's process and scientific results over God, the creator of the world, and all humans, including Darwin himself. If Darwin's theory was so powerful and convincing, why couldn't he prove where the more primitive species had come from? Darwin believed that all mammals such as apes and humans evolved from the earlier existing mammal from the beginning of time. The question is, why aren't people still evolving from mammals? Why aren't children born and evolving now? The challenge in Darwinism theory is that people agree with it? It goes to show what kind of world we live in when people just believe anything someone tells them.

Do you really believe that Darwin was the only man with this kind of belief? Of course not! They still exist today all around us. In evolution, there is no spiritual thinking. Because of Darwin's education and intellect, others were convinced that Darwin was correct. Be cautious of someone that has a charismatic and controlling way. Usually this kind of person does not have a relationship with Jesus Christ. Therefore, you are walking into a trap and can be doomed for destruction.

If evolution were true, where does the love of God fit in? Where is God in evolution period? God is all powerful and sovereign over all things. He is the Creator, not Darwin. Darwin's belief does not even line up with the word of God. 1 Corinthians 6:19-20 says our body is the temple of God and He dwells inside. Evolution is unable to explain God sovereignty and omnipotence.

I wish Darwin would have met great men like: Moses, Abraham, Isaac and Jacob, Joseph, Elijah, the Apostle Paul, John the Baptist, King David and the Prophet Samuel. Darwin does not believe that God created man. They believed that aliens altered human existence. They really did not understand the genetic and human makeup. Some believe that this alteration was a game of intelligence, altering human beings. There is a gene in our bodies that is reasonable and strictly for communication in our genetic codes. The problem with evolution is that it can't explain God's communication system. Evolutionist still can't explain God's patterns of numbers or system of order. Evolutionists are unable to explain life from God's view.

Be careful of what you believe because you are impressed by a charismatic man. Jim Jones killed hundreds of people because his charismatic style lured them in to drinking poison. That was the act of Satan!

The origin of homosapiens originated in African according to scientists. The word homosapiens mean wise man, thinking man, rational man, and knowing man. It is the species name for humans, sometimes referred to as anatomically modern humans. Anatomically refers to a bodily structure. It also means of or relating to the anatomy. This discovery was in Africa.

Adam and Eve in the Hebrew book of Genesis is the only obvious answer to man being on the earth and the population beginning. DNA is a huge factor. God wants us to know where we originated and that our identity is with God. The Apostle wants each person to know that your body is a temple of the Holy Spirit. Your body is not yours. Your body belongs to the God who created you. The way you treat your body sends a message to God that you either care or do not care about your temple. Ask God to help you take care of your body, the temple where the Spirit dwells. You were purchased with a price. It was Jesus giving His on body to die for yours. You were made by God to live a holy and righteous life before God.

We are in a sense like Samson. He was born for a purpose. He was not to drink wine, nor cut his hair. Your body is precious to God? You have work to do in the Kingdom! Your temple is designed to praise and worship God. Your body (the temple) is a spirit carrier! You walk with God's spirit inside of your temple. You were created to worship Him every day of your life. If you are born again as stated in Romans 10:9-10 and baptized (Matthew 28:19-22), God wants you to know that you are complete in His temple to dwell in Him. God is a jealous God. So be aware that enemy still wants to steal, kill and destroy. Jesus said, "that no one will snatch them out of His hand (John 10:28-30)."

Questions:

1. Who said that your body is a temple of the Holy Spirit?

_____
_____

2. Why is your body a Temple of the Holy Spirit?
_____
_____

3. What is a temple?

_____
_____
_____

4. Since your body is a temple, what will you do different?

_____
_____
_____

CHAPTER 19

GOD IS LOVE

1 John 4:16 And so we know and rely on the love God has for us. God is love. Whoever lives in love lives in God, and God in them.

God is the very existence of love and all love stems from Him. We rely on God's love. (1 John 4:8) His love never misses an area that needs attention. Jesus will never leave you nor forsake you! His love is my global positioning system. He will help you find love when you need it. His love is positioned in the right place in your heart and throughout your spirit and soul. If you are challenged by anything in your life, turn to God. If you are lonely or have medical Issues, God will be there for you. Even if you have problems maintaining your faith, there is nothing more powerful than Jesus love. It is already extended to you right now. Call on His name. He knows all about your every decision. Don't let anyone put you down. Don't let anyone tell you that you are anything less than a blessed child of the living God. Your identity has changed! If anyone put you down it was a lie from the devil. Rebuke it in Jesus name! Then get on with walking in blessings and favor in your life. You are a child of God! The love of God positioned you to receive His love and favor daily! Walk in it! Lift your head up with high confidence and power in Jesus name! You are a victor that has overcome all enemies in Jesus name!

Today, cast down every high imagination and the bondages

that have been trying to destroy you. Turn your heart to the Son of God, Jesus Christ Cast down all enemies that try to keep you from Jesus. Do not accept the evil voice that tries to convince you to stay out of God's presence, away from the church and from the saints. Block the enemy out by calling on Jesus for help. Call Jesus name at least seven times. Repeat this: In Jesus name, I am clean, and I am free. I am made whole and my life is worth living. In Jesus name, my marriage is strong, and we love each other. In Jesus name, we will honor each other and submit to each other. We will be intimate as much as the Lord allows. I am rich in my inheritance! All my bad habits are gone. I am a new creature in Christ Jesus. Lord Jesus, I repent of my sins today! Jesus, I believe confess that you are the Son of God. You died for my sins on the cross and on the third day you rose from the dead with all power and authority in your hand by your Father in heaven. Come into my heart and keep me as one of your children. I accept you as Lord and Savior in my life from this day on. Lord, also continue to strengthen my marriage. All praise, glory, and honor go to your name O' Lord.

CRUCIFIED FOR THE SAKE OF LOVE

ROMANS 6:6 knowing this, that our old man was crucified with Him, that the body of sin might be done away with, that we should no longer be slaves of sin.

A strong mind is for those who have discovered God's power. They have identified the enemy and have not allowed him to rule over their mind, body, soul and spirit (1 Thessalonians 5:23). What is Jesus speaking through the Apostle? He is informing us that if we are believers in Jesus, our old man must be crucified. This applies to all believers. Therefore, the devil and his demons cannot break your mind or spirit because you stand on the solid Rock of Jesus. The only way you can crucify the flesh is to submit to God and resist the devil. When you have crucified the flesh (those worldly thoughts), then you will have a strong mind in Jesus Christ. A strong Godly mind is in those whose thoughts are governed by the Holy Spirit. This person trusts in God and knows how to get on with their life, regardless of those that hate, disrespect or turn their back on them. The indication of a sound mind in Jesus is someone who can think in the spirit and think logically or naturally. They are led by the Holy Spirit. Don't be fooled! Ask yourself if you are living an undercover life of sin. You are if you are doing things that you think no one else sees you doing. The devil has your life in his hand. You can get on your knees and ask Jesus to come into your heart right now! You are being set up by the devil for a great fall and it will impact your family. Make the right choice now in the name of Jesus! Come out of darkness! The devil does not care who you are. You can have a perfectly happy marriage and the enemy can still come in like a storm and rip it apart, especially if you are not rooted in Jesus Christ. He rips those apart who are weak within themselves. You need a relationship with Jesus Christ today.

He died baring the sins of the world. As a result, he defeated death, the grave, and hell. His crucifixion accesses eternal love, joy, and peace for us. He wants us to maintain ourselves until He returns. Read 1 Thessalonians 5:23 May God himself, the God of peace, sanctify you through and through. May your whole spirit, soul and body be kept blameless at the coming of our Lord Jesus Christ?

A FATHER'S LOVE

LUKE 15:15-23 Then he went and joined himself to a citizen of that country, and he sent him into his fields to feed swine. And he would gladly have filled his stomach with the pods that the swine ate, and no one gave him *anything*. "But when he came to himself, he said, 'How many of my father's hired servants have bread enough and to spare, and I perish with hunger! I will arise and go to my father, and will say to him, "Father, I have sinned against heaven and before you, and I am no longer worthy to be called your son. Make me like one of your hired servants."'" "And he arose and came to his father. But when he was still a great way off, his father saw him and had compassion, and ran and fell on his neck and kissed him. And the son said to him, 'Father, I have sinned against heaven and in your sight, and am no longer worthy to be called your son.' "But the father said to his servants, 'Bring out the best robe and put *it* on him, and put a ring on his hand and sandals on *his* feet. And bring the fatted calf here and kill *it,* and let us eat and be merry

This story is powerful because it is a display and symbol of a true father's love for His Son. It also shows a powerful scene of how a son can be so lost and disrespectful to his father. My biological father was my hero period. He has always had the ultimate respect from me as a son. I credit him for everything. He set the example in so many ways. None of us would show such arrogance and disrespect like this prodigal son in the story. We had the ultimate respect for our biological Father. Nevertheless, when we made mistakes or veered off the path, he knew exactly what to do. If it were the same situation, he would have welcomed us home as well.

Here is the essential point in this story. Our Father in heaven always has His arms open for any of His children to come back home. You can come back home to Jesus today and not be left out in the world for enemy to destroy your life. If you ran from God, you can come back to his open arms of love. He is the only one (without a doubt) that will not turn you away. He will not look at you any differently or cast a negative judgment on you. He desires that you come and receive His love. You will be restored and blessed when you receive His love. You will be made new in Jesus Christ when you receive His love. You will become an overcomer. There are multiple advantages in Jesus Christ when you receive His love. Do not miss out.

There are several demonstrations of love in the Bible of the Father in heaven showing love to His children. However, in this story, the Lord shows us what happens when a beloved son drifts away from the key source in his life, which is His father; and chooses to live in the world. In this case, the son exhausted every resource he had on hand. He even reached the limits of his prideful way of thinking. Pride only takes you so far in a manner of pretense and lies. It is easy for a human being to walk out of love into a prideful attitude and behavior.

Questions & Discussion

Why did the son leave home?
_____
_____

What did the son experience?
_____
_____

What did the father do when his son returned home?
_____
_____

Who does this father remind you of? Why?
_____
_____
_____

What would you do in a similar experience or this case?
_____
_____
_____

THE CITY OF GOD

Revelation 21:15-21 The angel who talked to me held in his hand a gold measuring stick to measure the city, its gates, and its wall. When he measured it, he found it was a square, as wide as it was long. In fact, its length and width and height were each 1,400 miles. Then he measured the walls and found them to be 216 feet thick (according to the human standard used by the angel). The wall was made of jasper, and the city was pure gold, as clear as glass. The wall of the city was built on foundation stones inlaid with twelve precious stones: the first was jasper, the second sapphire, the third agate, the fourth emerald, the fifth onyx, the sixth carnelian, the seventh chrysolite, the eighth

beryl, the ninth topaz, the tenth chrysoprase, the eleventh jacinth, the twelfth amethyst. The twelve gates were made of pearls—each gate from a single pearl! And the main street was pure gold, as clear as glass.

This is a city prepared out of love for God's people. Our Father lives in Heaven. He also lives inside of each Christian. Those who have come into God's family have a permanent home awaiting them called heaven. If there are things hindering you, let it go and get prepared for eternal life with our Lord, Jesus. This city is made by God! It's a holy city, New Jerusalem, with streets of gold, gates made of a single pearl. Jesus said in Revelation 21:3 the tabernacle of God is here. Jesus is the light of this city (Isaiah 60:19). Listen, your life does not end on this earth. You live forever and reign with God. God awaits your arrival if you are one of His because He knows where you will end up. Nevertheless, you must be born again (John 3:3). Don't miss out on this blessing. Saints of the Most High God will be according to 1 Thessalonians 4:16-18, caught up in the air with our Lord return for those who love Him. Christian bodies will be glorified bodies in Jesus Christ. Why am I telling you this? It is because you need to know the facts and you need to have hope and trust in God for His plan for your life. The other reason is because I am reminding you in this book of the power God use to demonstrate maxing out His love, yet never exhausting any of His love for all His people. Do you belong to God? Do you have salvation? Did you accept Jesus inside God's church on Sunday morning (Romans 10:9)? Did you get baptized like Jesus commanded us (Matthew 28)? Listen, if you fall into this category of Revelation 21:8, you will not enter if you have not repented of your sin. Stop living the destructive life and live for Jesus Christ, the author and finisher of our faith. You can do it right now in Jesus name! Remember, all men will be judged on that great day. Therefore, surrender to Jeus so that your name will be written in the book of life (Revelations 21:27).

ABOUT THE AUTHOR

Joseph Harris is the Pastor and Founder of Christian Worship Outreach Center Ministries. His mission is to preach the Gospel of Jesus Christ! Pastor Harris is Kingdom Focused! His primary focus and foundation is the word of God. He is a Soul Winner and Kingdom Builder. He delights in introducing others to receive Jesus Christ, as Lord and Savior.

Pastor Harris is a husband and father. He is also the author of several other books: Transformation Man, Man Under Construction, Rock the Pedestal, Fallen Scales, Reverse the Tide, The God Hold On Me, and The God Runner.

REFERENCES

Clarke, Adam. "Commentary on 1 Samuel 7:12". "The Adam Clarke Commentary". https://www.studylight.org/commentaries/acc/1-samuel-7.html. 1832.

Dobson E.G., Feinberg, C.L., Hindson, E.E. Kroll, W. M., & Wilmington H.L., (1994). Parallel Bible Commentary. *The complete King James Verson*, p 2438.

www.ingramcontent.com/pod-product-compliance
Lightning Source LLC
Chambersburg PA
CBHW071434160426
43195CB00013B/1891